Suzanne

A house is a place...

Home is a sta...

mind

Welcome Home

Merry Christmas 95

Maureen

Daniel

# HOME

# HOME

*American Writers
Remember Rooms of Their Own*

EDITED BY
SHARON SLOAN FIFFER
AND STEVE FIFFER

PANTHEON BOOKS   NEW YORK

Copyright © 1995 by Sharon Sloan Fiffer and Steve Fiffer

All rights reserved under International and Pan-American
Copyright Conventions. Published in the United States by
Pantheon Books, a division of Random House, Inc., New York,
and simultaneously in Canada by Random House of
Canada Limited, Toronto.

"Storm Door" was originally published in *Farmer's Market*.
The Afterword was originally published in *HG*.

Grateful acknowledgment is made to *Alfred A. Knopf, Inc.* and *Viking*
for permission to reprint an excerpt from *Colored People* by Henry
Louis Gates, Jr., copyright © 1994 by Henry Louis Gates, Jr. Rights
in the British Commonwealth are administered by Viking, London.
Reprinted by permission of Alfred A. Knopf, Inc. and Viking,
a division of Penguin UK.

Library of Congress Cataloging-in-Publication Data

Home : American writers remember rooms of their own / edited
by Sharon Sloan Fiffer and Steve Fiffer.
p. cm.
ISBN 0-679-44206-5
1. Authors, American—20th century—Homes and haunts. 
2. Authors,
American—20th century—Childhood and youth. 3. Rooms.
4. Home.
I. Fiffer, Sharon Sloan, 1951– . II. Fiffer, Steve.
PS141.H545 1995
818´.540308355—dc20
95-14809
CIP

*Book design by M. Kristen Bearse*
*Illustrations by Laurie Jo Neary/Seed Time Studio*
*Cover photograph by Sally Gall*

Manufactured in the United States of America
First Edition
2  4  6  8  9  7  5  3  1

# CONTENTS

# INTRODUCTION:
## FROM THE SIXTH STAIR

## SHARON SLOAN FIFFER

When I was a child, my parents moved three times. Between ages two and eighteen, I lived in four different houses. I don't remember the brick bungalow on Bourbonnais Avenue, although I must have taken my first steps, spoken my first words there. I couldn't tell you much about the three-bedroom tract house on Western Hills Drive or the small brick ranch on Hawkins Street, where my mother still lives. I can, however, conjure up the floor plan, the fleur-de-lis wallpaper, and the maple early American furniture of the Cape Cod on Cobb Boulevard—the only house I ever called *home*.

My father found a shabby six-room house that was going to be torn down to make way for a new bridge over the Kankakee River. It wasn't a landmark—although it was as old as the town—or a renovator's dream—even with its oak flooring and period wainscoting. It was just small and cheap, so he bought it and had it moved to a small piece of property between two grand old houses on Kankakee's fanciest street, Cobb Boulevard.

The neighbors on either side of our lot had gardened in it for years, growing flowers, vegetables, and fruit trees. One morning, our house was hauled up to the curb, and dropped onto a newly dug-out basement and poured foundation right in the middle of their Eden. When asparagus and rhubarb came up in our backyard later in the spring, my brother and I ran to our mother screaming that Mrs. Householter was picking plants out of our yard.

"Let her take it," my mother said, looking out the kitchen window. "She planted it."

My parents owned a tavern called the E Z Way Inn and together worked long, hard hours—my father tending bar and keeping the books, my mother making pots of soup and grilling hamburgers for the Roper Stove factory workers who poured in the door at noon. Mr. Householter, our new neighbor to the north, was a lawyer, and Mr. Henry, to our south, was a retired insurance company executive. Their wives stayed at home.

There weren't many young children around. Malcolm Moore was my age and lived down the street. His father was a doctor, and they had a real goldfish pond in their backyard. My mother saw me leaning over examining the water lilies one day and forbid me to return there to play.

"Somebody will push you in and you'll drown," she told me, sure that our more established and respectable neighbors despised us that much.

Next door, Nora Householter, five years older than I, took

pity on me. I'm sure now that there were many days she regretted allowing me to become her shadow—like the day that I crashed her birthday party—but she never banished me. I don't even remember an unkind word. What I do remember was her imagination, her dreams, her ambitions. She made plans. She started a detective agency so we could solve neighborhood crimes. She dressed me in costumes and paraded me around the neighborhood. She tested food on me. I was the one who tasted the sour milk, the moldy cake. I was her jester, her slave, her pupil.

She taught me everything I knew then, and most of what I remember today. Once she told me that a boy in her class was a brain—so smart he didn't even have to think—and I told her that Sister Rose Cicely had said that I was the smartest girl in the second grade so I must be a brain too.

"No, Sharon," she said, staring hard into my eyes. "You're a good reader, which is fine, but not the same as being a brain."

The most important thing she taught me was to listen. She taught me this, in part, by having so much to say herself, so much interesting information, so many ideas and colors in her head that I couldn't not listen. But she also taught me to listen because she asked questions. She wanted to know everything, and she taught me that if you want to know everything you have to ask and you have to listen. I wanted to please her. I wanted to entertain her, so I needed answers to her questions. Where would I get them? I was seven years old, a good reader maybe, but no brain, and I hadn't read anything that she hadn't read. I needed my own stories.

That's when I fell in love with our house and its perfect layout. My bedroom was upstairs next to my parents' room. My brother, seven years older than I, had a downstairs room, off the dining room. I remember worrying whether, when we first moved in, he felt left out, alone at night on the first floor. Later I realized that a ground-level window for late-night exits and entrances was far more important than being close to Mom and Dad in case you had a nightmare.

In any case, I was glad that he was downstairs. It meant that when I was put to bed at eight, no one would be coming up the stairs until much later. My parents were night people. Television people. They watched the news, they watched movies, they watched Jack Paar, they fell asleep under newspapers in the living room. And our television was well placed, as are all good shrines, for maximum visibility, in the northwest corner of the living room, the corner directly across from the stairs that led up to my bedroom. In fact, six steps down from the top was the best seat in the house. From that stair, one could see the television, look down on the top of my father's head in his pre–Lazy Boy "easy" chair, read the headlines of the newspaper he was holding (mid–school year, after I got the glasses I desperately needed, I could read whole articles), hear every living-room "adult" conversation, all lectures to my older brother before he was sent to his room, and yet—and this was most important—I could not be seen. A foundation pillar that came right up on the side of the steps made a window frame for me to sit behind. If I leaned back, I was invisible to those sitting below.

I didn't have to lean back very often. Any illusionist will tell you that people rarely notice what they don't expect to see. Because I was a good girl, obedient and self-reliant, my parents never expected me to say good night from under my covers, count to sixty five times, then creep down six steps and settle in for the next few hours on what I came to think of as "my stair."

Some nights my parents didn't talk. My father read three newspapers then—the *Chicago Tribune* to see what the Republicans thought, the *Chicago Sun Times* to see what the Democrats thought, and the *Kankakee Daily Journal* to see who died—and I tried to read over his shoulder. Even an advanced reader like myself found it impossible to decipher "Voice of the People" essays or figure out why a comic strip was called "Steve Roper" when there was never anybody named Steve Roper in the stories. It was easier to watch television, memorizing the jokes that received the most laughter so I could repeat them to Nora.

Nora liked the jokes and the bits of popular culture I offered, but what she really loved were my word-for-word, blow-by-blow accounts of the battles between my fourteen-year-old brother and my parents. Emory was what I as a parent would now call "creative and imaginative," seeking his own identity and rebelling against conformity. At least that's how I explain my own child's Emory-like behavior. My father, however, lacking a college degree and the bookshelf of today's anxious parents, called him a pathological liar. Dad would put down his papers and listen patiently while Emory explained why he needed five dollars or why Mom and Dad might be getting a call the next day about an absence from English class or why he needed to spend the night at a friend's to study for a big test. My father would usually nod and sigh, then ask a few pertinent questions, which would lead to a few contradictory answers, which would lead to demand for full disclosure, which might or might not come only after much wrangling, yelling, and swearing from all concerned.

Occasionally my mother would shush everyone: "For God's sake, be quiet, you'll wake up Sharon!"

I'd lean back, but no one even glanced up. "Don't worry, Nellie, she sleeps through everything," my dad would shout and go back to the argument at hand.

I'd reconstruct the entire scene for Nora the next day. I punctuated my story with some of my dad's sighs. I'd mop my brow and screw the heels of my hands into my eyes and groan, "Emory, for once in your life, just tell me the goddamn truth," and Nora would howl with laughter. I learned to edit out the boring parts; the nights when my dad simply handed my brother a five-dollar bill and said, "Fine, here you go," were hardly interesting enough to merit retelling. I took what I knew would work and put it up front. I embellished. I ended my version at an edgy middle moment, rather than let it spin out into the same old family argument denouement. I made our family stories funnier, richer, and deeper—all to get Nora to sit on the porch with me a little longer, to make her laugh a little harder, and to regard me more and more as an equal.

The frame through which I watched my own family made them real to me—they weren't reacting to me as mother, father, and brother. I wasn't even in the picture. I saw them as whole people, unique. They carried around all the baggage that comes with working twelve-hour days and still trying to be a father, the perfect housewife; I even saw both sides of my brother, Emory—struggling to grow up and be cool and be a son and be a student and be a friend and be a brother. My vantage point allowed me to see the way all people struggle when they talk, when they argue—they try to listen, be fair, but mostly they want to be understood themselves. They want to be recognized. They want to make sense.

That's my house memory. Oh, there are others, which still make the hair stand up on the back of my neck. I can perfectly recall the sensation of lying on the living-room carpet six inches from the face of the oscillating fan, reading comic books: the overwhelming heat, then the rush of air as the fan passed, then the heat, then the air, heat, air. That was summer.

Then there was the cardboard red brick mantel my parents assembled each December. Every year I tried to hang a stocking on it for Santa to fill, every year the mantel fell, knocking over the light with the rotating red and orange filter that was supposed to simulate firelight, and every year my mother would come in screaming, "Are you trying to start a real fire? Do you want to burn the house down?" That was winter.

But the stairs were all seasons in the house on Cobb Boulevard. I learned to listen and to tell stories sitting on that sixth stair. The frame of pillar and wall was my magic slate then, what my computer screen is now. I learned what made my parents laugh. I found out that what my parents said to my brother and what they said to each other afterward were two different and often opposite things. I heard my parents fight, I saw my father cry. I learned to swear. I developed a sense of family and friendship and parenthood and childhood. I discovered home.

It is our place on the stairs or the front porch, or in the bedroom, the garage, or Dad's workshop where he kept his tools through which we connect our visions of home—what it was or wasn't, what it is or what it can be. Home might be contained within four walls or it might be a vision of the night sky from a back-yard swing set, a windowsill with our mother's African violets, a double-wide trailer with a pull-out bed, or the powdery smell of our grandmother's apartment.

The eighteen writers who share memories of home here—room by room, memory by memory—do so with humor, with truth, with an open heart. The home created between the covers of this book is one in which we, writers and readers, are all welcome—universal, real, filled with specific detail, perfect and imperfect recall. It is the act of writing, reading, and remembering our own homes—the smells from the kitchen, the whispers from the bedroom, the sliver of light at the bottom of a closed door—that brings us together. It is what brings us home.

We invite you to pull up your most comfortable chair or curl up under your favorite quilt or stretch out on your stoop or prop up your feet on a kitchen chair. Just as I told my tales to Nora Householter all those years ago to bind her to me in friendship, the writers tell their tales to you. Stay. Listen. Remember.

# HOME

# RICHARD BAUSCH

1961

We arrive in an uproar of summer voices, piling out of our new Ford, with its tale fins that are smaller than last year's, and its wraparound windshield. Our father sells cars, now—has done so since late 1957, when he left his job with the Agriculture Department against the advice of his parents and almost everyone else he knew—and we have grown accustomed to having the latest models to ride around in. There are six of us—the girls, Barbara and Betty, eighteen and fourteen, respectively; the twins, Bobby and me, sixteen only two months ago; and the babies, as we call them—Steve, who is ten, and Tim, who is six.

The babies are too young to understand what this visit is really about.

We have come to my mother's family home in Washington,

D. C., a big Victorian house on a shady street near Catholic University. Cousins and aunts and uncles greet us from the wide lawn, with its big overspreading trees, its tattered patches of brightness and shade. Barbara, a young woman now, leads the babies through everyone, accepting the kisses and the teasings. Bobby follows them, with his hands in his pockets and his head down; he's a pool shark. Very cool. The aunts and uncles call him "the bad one," meaning it as a joke; and of course, being sixteen, he has taken it deeply, and with pain, to heart. He wears pointy-toed Italian shoes and tight peg-legged pants, a white shirt, and a dark vest. His dark red hair is combed high, and then pulled down in the center of his forehead. He walks around the side of the big house to the long backyard, where the men are throwing horseshoes. I watch him go. I'm a basketball player—quite good at it, in fact. We are identical twins, but we do not have a lot to say to each other these days; we don't even have the same friends. I wear white slacks, a blue shirt with the sleeves rolled up. My hair is combed something like Ricky Nelson's. I'm devout, and bookish (Bobby is also bookish, but he hides it better), and everyone knows I'm planning for the priesthood. I'm "the good one," which I have also taken to heart, though without being quite conscious of it. Bob and Helen are our parents—in their young forties, with a big family growing up on them, and more money than they are accustomed to having. They are in love, after almost twenty years of marriage, and they know it.

Together, they walk across the wide lawn to the house, carrying gifts. This is Minnie Roddy's eightieth birthday. Helen is Minnie's granddaughter, and was for the most part raised by her.

Helen's father died in the great flu epidemic of 1918, and she never knew him. Her mother, Louise, had to go to work for the District, as the adults put it, meaning Washington. So Minnie Roddy and her sister, Daisy, raised Helen, and after Louise married Dick Underwood, and little Florence came along, they raised her, too. Dick Underwood is a man with a tendency to let the bottle get the best of him; he is always going and coming, in and out of the family's good graces. By 1961, it has been several years since I've seen him; I remember that he had a big car, and thousands of books. Even more than the many at our own house in the suburbs, twenty minutes away.

One lost summer day when Bobby and I were very small, Dick Underwood pulled up in front of the house in the big car and asked us if we wanted to go for a little ride. It was a long, low-to-the-ground tan convertible, and the top was down. The shine on it gave us back ourselves as sharply as if we had been gazing in a beige mirror. We climbed in, excited and happy, and very impressed by him, and with a laugh deep in his throat he swung out into the road. We felt the breeze moving over us, and we looked at the brightly polished dashboard with all its interesting dials and buttons and vents. He drove past the anti-aircraft guns of Fort Myer, and on out into the Virginia countryside. He let us stand and face into the wind. At one point, he said, "Guess we better get on back, because I've got to wee." We laughed helplessly at this, since we had never heard an adult use the word.

When we pulled in front of the house, perhaps half an hour later, Helen came out into the front yard and chased him away. "Don't you ever come back here," she shouted.

Later, Helen learned from her mother, Louise, that he came

back home and walked up onto the porch and began to cry. "That daughter of yours doesn't like me much," he said.

We were not told any of this at the time, of course.

At sixteen, I know it, though, as I know that Louise has recently suffered a kind of breakdown. I am grown up enough to have gleaned this knowledge, even as my parents have been fairly close-mouthed about it. I am aware of this gathering of the family as a celebration, but also as a means to offer support and comfort to one of its number. Grandmother Louise is seated in the porch swing now, looking like herself to me as I climb the steps of the porch.

"Come here," she says, reaching for me. She is dark, with deep-socketed eyes and prominent cheekbones. There are photographs in the foyer of this big house that show how beautiful she was in 1921, and '31, and '41. Her arms are thinner than I recall, and her voice is a note lower, it seems. She puts her arms around me, and I pat her bony shoulders. Next to her in the swing is Aunt Daisy. Eighty-four, big-shouldered, with heavy arms and spotted skin, and the rounded features of some other branch of the Roddy clan, she is a kindly woman with a strange bluntness about her. Her directness is something I try to avoid always, and am seldom able to.

Now she says, "Louise, let someone else get a hug."

Louise lets go of me. I walk into Aunt Daisy's heavy arms. "When you gonna get some meat on your bones?" she says.

This has become a favorite question of hers, and of course I have no answer to it. "I don't know," I say. The universal child-

hood dodge, and I feel vaguely resentful for having been drawn
into it: I want to think of myself as an adult now. I am old enough
to drive a car, and my father occasionally lets me have a glass of
beer. I smoke—though they do not know this yet.

"You're a good boy," Louise says, patting my shoulders as if
to test the muscles. "Nice broad shoulders. I have such handsome
grandchildren."

"He's too skinny, if you ask me," says Aunt Daisy.

Louise says, "No one asked you."

"I said if you did," Aunt Daisy says.

I step back and let the others greet her and Louise—who
wants to see the babies. Somewhere nearby, I hear the sound of
baseball being announced on a radio. The Senators are playing
the hated Yankees, and Roger Maris has just hit another home
run; he's far ahead of Ruth's pace, and is leaving Mantle behind
too. Now and again, there's the clang of the horseshoes hitting
the iron stake out back. Someone shouts my older sister's name.
"Barbara, Barbara."

"Where's Minnie?" my mother asks.

"Inside," says Aunt Daisy. "She baked some things for the
children."

The wind moves the shade on the grass here in front of the
house, where two cousins are lobbing a ball back and forth. I
want to take part in this, yet I'm also now interested in what's
being said between my father and Louise. His tone is almost the
same as the one he uses with us when he means to discipline us.
"You're never as alone as you think you are, Weezy. You ought to
try remembering that."

"I couldn't feel it," Louise says. "Couldn't feel a thing."

"But you know it. Don't you. We're all with you, everywhere you go. Why don't you pick up the phone and call somebody."

"Couldn't make myself do anything."

"She needs a good rest," Aunt Daisy says.

Louise says, "Not that kind of rest, Daisy."

"Don't put words in my mouth."

"Not everything has to do with working too hard—that's all I meant. Rest doesn't solve everything. It has nothing to do with loneliness, for instance."

"Well, we're all here now," says my father. "No reason for anybody to feel alone."

"You feel whatever comes," Louise says. "Or whatever refuses to come." Her voice is calm, almost casual. She looks right at me, and I am oddly aware that there are angles of bone in her face that are like my mother's, and mine. For some reason, I think of death, of the dark Irish I heard Uncle Charles talking about one afternoon earlier in this summer, when the first inklings of the trouble came through to me. I have been thinking a lot of death, too, lately. And abruptly, I sense some stream of propensity flowing into me from this thin, nervous woman with her shadowed eyes. At the time, of course, I am unable to express this feeling, even to myself. I have no words, only the slight chill of recognizing my own face in her face. I go down off the porch and out into an afternoon of games—tag, baseball, horseshoes.

Toward evening, I go up on the porch again, and stand gazing out at the ramshackled, flat-roofed building across the street. Clumps of grass have pushed up through the blue gravel in front of it, and a slab of concrete looks as though it's crumbling away into the weeds just beyond the side door. I have no idea what this building is (perhaps it was once a gas station?), but it interests me, since it is so clearly abandoned. Beyond it, on a raised and well kept bed of darker-blue gravel, is a railroad track. I have been told many times that I am not to cross the streets. But I am sixteen now, and I consider that I've reached the age of being able to decide for myself. I know that sooner or later all the adults will go inside, and I will thus have a chance to go over and put my hands down on the cold iron, and think of the train. I might even watch one come through, though in all the times I have been to this house, I have no memory of ever seeing one.

So I wait on the porch, and the adults do go inside, my grandmother leaning on my father's arm. Everyone, that is, except Aunt Daisy, who sits in the swing and moves just enough to make the chains squeak. I'm only partially aware of the sound, standing with my bony elbows on the railing, gazing out across the shade and sun.

"What're you day-dreaming about?" Aunt Daisy asks me.

I turn to look at her. She's at the other end of the porch, a distance. The wide, shaded expanse seems momentarily to shift, as though I have faltered at the perception of its size. "I was hoping to see a train go by," I say.

She glances out at the street, her street. She has lived here for thirty years. She nods. "They come by at night, and very early in the morning."

"I don't think I've ever seen one come by."

"You just don't remember. We had to go over there and get your brother and you one time. You were both sitting on the bank on the other side of the track, up high in those weeds, and when the train came through it stopped, and you were stuck there. You both started crying. The whole street heard the noise you two made."

I strain to remember this, and can't.

"You don't remember."

"No ma'am," I say.

"What're you going to do with yourself?"

"Ma'am?" I say.

"You're almost grown. You going to be an artist, like your mother?"

Aunt Daisy has seen my drawings, and it is only recently that I have been informed that the pastels on the living-room wall— of Christ in the garden, of people in a rainy street—are Helen's work, done while she was still in high school. They are all so much better than my own, so much more complete, startlingly exact and true to life. There are more of them in the piano bench, and in various places about the house—something they have all taken for granted. Helen herself merely smiles at the plain astonishment of her children at this thing she has done better than any of them, without ever letting them know when she appreciated their meager efforts how far from her own drawings they were.

"Well?" Aunt Daisy says. "Are you going to be an artist?"

"I don't know," I say. "I guess so."

We're quiet. In a few moments, the big tan convertible pulls up, years older but just as waxed and polished and new-looking, and Dick Underwood gets out. He comes across the lawn, looking very natty, in two-tone shoes and a beige three-piece suit. He's smoking a cigar.

"Daisy," he says, coming up onto the porch.

"When you gonna quit that smelly cigar," Daisy says.

"Sometime," he tells her. He looks at me. "Hey, boy."

At the door, Louise's Uncle Charles, with his own cigar, says, "Well, you made it after all."

"Charley."

The screen door opens, and Dick Underwood goes on inside. I hear my mother greet him in the foyer of the house, as everyone else does. "Helen," he says distinctly over the voices of the others. "Where's the birthday girl?"

"In the kitchen," my mother says.

I hear him wish Minnie Roddy a happy birthday. And I hear him ask Louise how she is feeling.

"Sometimes," Aunt Daisy says to me, "the trains don't come for days. It's just a switching track now, I think."

"A what?"

She gets up from the swing and walks to me, slow, in her odd, thick-heeled shoes. She takes my elbow and leads me to the edge of the stairs, and points at the tracks. "They use it to switch cars. They come part way, then go back—part way and back, that's all. It has something to do with the station, which is over there. But up on that side of the track, that hill over there, is where you and your brother were."

I follow her hand with my eyes, and even amid the noise and confusion coming from the rooms behind us her gesture seems to promise some tranquilizing effect on everything, as if she has raised her hand to ask for quiet from the world. Indeed it all does seem to pause. And in that pause I receive a visceral sense of how it is in life—I will never be able to explain this any more directly than to say that in that moment I am aware that there is trouble

and that somehow in this casual gesture of Aunt Daisy's, showing me where I once was separated from this house by the huge
noise and clatter of a train, she gives me the strongest bodily impression of where we leave off, and the rest of the world begins.

"You see?" she says. "Do you remember now?"

I do not. Yet the feeling that where we are standing is the
edge of our world has stopped my breath.

"Son?" she says.

"Yes ma'am," I say.


A little later, I'm sitting on the top step with a palm full of salt.
The dinner has been served—hamburgers and hot dogs from the
barbecue in back; potato salad and baked beans, deviled eggs,
ambrosia fruit salad, biscuits. The men are playing horseshoes in
back, and are letting Bobby play with them. He's holding his
own. I'm eating the salt, dipping my wet index finger into it, and
then putting the finger in my mouth. I have had part of a glass
of beer, and have experienced something of the frustration of
being too old to sit with the babies, and too young to sit with
the adults. I have argued with Bobby about the train—he claims
to remember quite well the incident of being caught on the
other side of the thing—and I'm filled with fear because, in the
casual conversation over dinner, my mother has mentioned that
she had the lump on her neck looked at.

We were all in the big lighted kitchen, sitting around the
white table when she said it, talking to her half sister, Florence.
"It's nothing," she said, "but a cyst."

"Are you going to have it removed?" Florence asked.

"We'll see. He said it was up to me."

"I think you should get it removed," said their mother, who sat with her hands folded on the tabletop, like someone waiting for a meeting to begin. She hadn't touched her food. And the conversation quickly shifted to attempts at getting her to eat.

"You don't eat enough to keep alive," Florence said.

And my father made a joke. "Guess we'll have to spoon it down you, Weezy, like it seems we just stopped doing with the babies."

"I'll eat, if everyone will stop watching me," Louise said.

A little later, crouched in the side yard with the cousins, I heard Peggy, the oldest cousin at nineteen, tell of an auto accident a friend of hers witnessed. "There was a man in the car, all crunched up and barely breathing and they worked for hours to get him out. The windshield was all smashed out and then somebody found a pair of shoes on the passenger side, and they realized there'd been another person in the car. So they started looking for this other person, and a man comes walking down the street toward them, kind of staggering, just in socks, and every little vein in his skin is bursting with blood, but the skin itself isn't broken. He was bright, bright red, just under the surface of the skin, and of course he was walking dead. Died before they got him in the ambulance. Not one break in the skin, and not a drop of blood on the ground."

Now, sitting on the porch eating the salt, I am trying to stop being afraid, trying not to think about dying or being so alone that you wanted to die, trying hard to trust my mother's casualness about the cyst. Minnie Roddy has come out and is in the swing, humming softly, fanning herself with part of the day's newspaper. She's got dark, metal-colored hair, kept close to her head by a net; she wears metal-framed glasses, small and square, and she looks like a smaller, more chiseled version of her daughter and granddaughter.

"You shouldn't eat salt like that," she says to me. "You'll get hardening of the arteries when you get older."

It seems to me that I have always understood the idea of growing older, though it nevertheless has felt impossible, something so far away as to be unimaginable, or nearly so. It feels quite present to me now, sitting here with the salt in my palm, hearing the squeak of the swing where Minnie Roddy sits.

Other children come up on the porch, led by Peggie and her sister Bitsy. The light is changing, the sun having moved to the other side of the house, beyond the tall roof with its towering chimneys and gabled dormers. The coolest place is here, in the shade, looking out at the darker green of the lawn with the massive shadow of the house in it. Children run in and out, younger than I, and of no interest to me. The screen door slaps to in its wooden frame, and the games these children are engaged in look to me now like the social life of another species. I am thinking of the dark that is coming—cysts, mental troubles, troubles with the bottle; old age and death. I don't want any of it. I want to go back to being a child, knowing nothing.

Aunt Daisy comes to the screen door and calls to all those who want cookies and ice cream.

Minnie Roddy says my name from the swing.

"Yes, ma'am," I say.

She pats the slats at her side in the swing. "Sit with me."

The others are running in the side yard, and out in front, too.

Hide-and-seek. The day's heat is diminishing slowly. She talks to me, telling me stories. She tells how Helen, walking down the hallway of Holy Cross High School at sixteen years of age, pinched the rear end of a cute, sandy-haired athlete who at that moment was talking to one of the nuns. The sandy-haired boy let out a shriek and startled the nun, who had no idea why a young man being told about his assignment having to do with *King Lear* should suddenly cry out like that. The young man was my father, of course, though Minnie doesn't say this; it's understood that I know. I laugh; I'm quite familiar with the story, but I love to hear it told. And then she begins talking of her husband, who left Ireland after killing a man in a fistfight in a pub. She has his picture, and I've seen it—a sharp-featured man with a shock of white hair and bushy white eyebrows, standing in bright sun, the eyes narrow, buried in a network of wrinkles. Minnie Roddy talks about when she met him, what she was wearing on that day in the last century, and her voice begins trailing off, as it has always done, as long as I have known her. I make an effort to listen, being polite, possessing no sense of her as having ever been anything but what she is: one of the old people, one of the stolid, warming presences of the house. She talks on, and soon my mother joins us, commenting about the cooling day, the fresh air, the good smell of the food. Others come out, Aunt Florence, Aunt Daisy, Uncle Charles, Dick Underwood, my father. My cousins Bitsy and Peggie, Aunt Marian and Uncle Francis, who made my father laugh against his will the first time they met and has been making him laugh ever since.

That first time was on this porch. An evening very much like this one, my father on a date with Helen, Marian on a date with

Francis. Minnie Roddy brought some small dishes of vanilla ice cream out for the young folks, and when she offered Francis's to him, he threw his arms up and made a sound of tremendous alarm and consternation, startling poor Minnie to the point of nearly falling backward into my father's lap.

"What in the world is wrong with you, young man?" Minnie said.

And Francis, still in the voice of someone quite alarmed, said, "Madam, I'll have you know I didn't even eat that stuff when I was poor."

My father tells this story again, and everyone, including Minnie, laughs at it again. Francis claims it's not true, but no one steps up to support him in this, least of all Minnie Roddy, who smiles tolerantly at him from the swing. Standing in the light of the open door are Louise and Dick Underwood, looking quite comfortable together, an old couple. Louise laughs at something one of the babies says about the bathtub upstairs, that it looks like it has real feet.

"Those are called claw feet," she says.

"They're scary," Helen says. "I always thought so when I was small."

"Nothing ever scared you," says her mother. "You climbed on a streetcar when you were three. Just toddled right up and got on."

"It's all that red hair," Dick Underwood says. "All that fire."

"Well," Uncle Charles says. "It's time."

A man has been hired to take a photograph. It has been decided that before we all sing "Happy Birthday" to Minnie, we'll have the photo taken. We are in the process of arranging ourselves, smaller children on the top steps of the porch, teenagers on the next ones down, adults on the descending steps, according to height. The photographer busily orchestrates this, running back and forth, trying to be efficient while entertaining and reassuring the smaller children. At length, in all the noise and bustle, he manages to get several shots, and in the next moment—before he can get the camera off its tripod—the group has scattered to all parts of the house and grounds.

Dusk is coming fast. Fireflies flicker everywhere in what looks like a perpetual rising motion, cinders lifting out of an invisible conflagration. There's the sound of the porch swing, and of the screen door slamming, and Minnie Roddy's small voice, talking. We sing "Happy Birthday," and she opens her gifts, with her bony, crooked fingers. I hear my mother's laugh above all the voices, and the fear closes in on me again. (This fear turns out to be groundless—and how strange, now, to think of it—the cyst is nothing more than that.) She's talking to Minnie about how she always loved to sit on this porch in the summer evenings, with everything so peaceful, and wait for my father to come walking down the street from one of his baseball games, still wearing his uniform, his glove hooked to his belt. All those wonderful times before the war.

"Happy birthday," she says to Minnie, and I can see that she's trying not to cry. But her face is all aglow in the light, and these are obviously tears of happiness. Some small element of this day has reassured her about her mother's trouble, and she is for the moment joyous, not dwelling on whatever else may be worrying her—the constant concern for her six children, and her husband, and everyone in her large, boisterous family. She kisses

Minnie on the cheek, then rises and says it's time to go. She asks me to help her gather everyone. I do. I'm the good one, remember. I fetch Bobby and the girls from the backyard, where they have been helping Bitsy catch fireflies; the babies are with Aunt Florence in the parlor, eating cookies. We all say our good-byes, kissing the aunts and uncles, and the cousins. Special care is taken that we all kiss Louise, who seems cheerful in a strangely hurried way, as if she's late for something, a little out of breath trying to catch up. Minnie Roddy, her mother, stands at her side, one hand on her shoulder. We wave at them from the new car, and then my father pulls us all away, and on into the falling summer night. I look back from the new car window at the light on that porch, the people standing there waving good-bye.

. . .

That was thirty-four years ago. Helen, in this memory, is more than five years younger than I am now. In the coming years, several people who posed for that photograph on the steps of the porch, including Minnie Roddy and Grandmother Louise, will die in her arms—she being the one of all of us who manages somehow not to let fear stop her from what she sees needs doing. With each of them she is patient, loving, practical.

Once, when bathing her dying father-in-law, she is lifting him and he looses his bowels. "I'm sorry," he says.

"Stop it," she tells him, quickly and efficiently cleaning it away. "Don't be silly." She kisses him on the forehead. He thanks her, and again she tells him not to be silly.

Through the years, she will talk of death as though it is something one has to do, a task, no more momentous than any other unpleasant task in its given time, a thing to get through and done with. She will go on to lose Barbara in an automobile accident—and her family, all her other children, will scatter to the four winds, will change, with families of their own. In 1985 she herself goes to sleep forever, cradled by her husband of so many years, so many houses and rooms; so many seasons with their attendant losses and delights, excitements and falterings, and the steady courage, the audaciousness and bravery and excellence of long love, the love that allows for every change, and itself does not change.

The big old family home is gone now. I have stood on the street where it once was, and recognized the railroad track, which is still there. The apartment building that occupies the ground where the house stood is dilapidated looking, running to seed itself. Yet, standing on that street, for a day-dreaming minute it is as if I can hear the voices of that summer afternoon and evening all those years ago, and I am once again standing on the steps of the porch with that feeling of being on a sort of promontory or precipice—that sense of the world out there, separate from this world here, with its familiar and so comfortably beloved sounds, even in the complication of fearing the changes I am just old enough to know are coming.

These decades later, I let the memory walk into me, through me. I greet it.

And I think how the house we live in now has its own wide porch, where my children watch storms and bask in the twilight warmth, and sing and slowly swing on the wooden swing, and, with me, raise their voices in one another's hearing—and where, on a lovely night five summers ago, one of the youngest of them,

Maggie, just two years old then, danced with my father, danced to the Benny Goodman music he has always loved so much, making a perfect end for a lovely day's celebration, of a new house, a new baby, Amanda Louise, and, as ever, the strength of this good family. And I think how, if the feeling is right and the love is as excellent and brave as it was when I was young, these children will carry the porch with them out into the harshness and turmoil of the world, and it will go on providing for them, even when they are far away, even when this house, too, is gone, and they have all come to see other places as the places they have for love and shelter.

Oh, welcome. Welcome.

# TONY EARLEY

## ONE

*The story goes like this:* my sister was born angry. She had colic as a newborn and cried for six weeks. After that, she just cried. We lived then with my grandparents in North Carolina. My father was away on temporary duty in the air force, and traveled the Western part of the country, installing radar systems. Mama did not want to be alone in a bad neighborhood in Texas with two babies in diapers. She and Granny stayed up with Shelly in shifts. Shelly wore them both out. Paw-paw could not stand to hear a baby cry. He was soft-hearted and nervous. He paced and smoked and sat and rocked on the porch. Shelly cried and cried. I was the only person in the house who slept much. I was fifteen months old, and had spent my life until then in small houses beneath the runway approaches of air force bases. Shelly had dark skin and black hair and eyes when she was born, but fair skin and blond hair and blue eyes by the time Daddy came back from TDY. He did not recognize her. She cried when he picked her up. Everyone agreed Shelly cried because she was mad, but could not figure out what she was mad about. It is said that the only thing that would make her stop crying in the morning was the sound of my grandfather's footsteps in the hallway.

## TWO

*Or this:* my great-grandmother kicked my great-grandfather out of their bed after my grandfather was born. My great-grandfather, Bill Ledbetter, slept in the hallway, near the front door, beside the steps leading upstairs. The hallway was unheated, and in the winter he slept under a great pile of quilts. In the summer he slept with the front and back doors open and lay comfortably in the breeze that traveled between the doors late at night.

One evening, during the Second World War, a Bible salesman stopped by the house. The house was close to no town, the road by it unpaved. Whole days went by without a car passing. The Bible salesman seemed particularly lost. He struggled with a heavy black suitcase. He was on foot, and did not speak English. It was near sundown. He made gestures with his hands and tried out strange words over and over. He looked from one uncomprehending face to another. My family had never heard anyone speak a foreign language. They could not tell what language it was. With hand signals Bill Ledbetter offered the Bible salesman a bed for the night. This was in a different time. He showed the Bible salesman a room upstairs. He motioned for the Bible sales-

man to open the suitcase. Bill Ledbetter looked inside and nodded at the Bibles he saw there and took the lamp and went back
downstairs.

That night the Bible salesman did not sleep. He paced the
floor of his room, from one side to the other, all night long.
Everyone downstairs listened. My mother was a little girl. She
climbed in bed with my grandparents. My uncle Tom crawled in
with my great-grandmother. My aunt Barbara wasn't born yet.
Everyone lay still in the dark and stared straight up while the
Bible salesman walked the floor above their heads. Bill Ledbetter got out of his bed, and very quietly took his shotgun down
from the hall tree. He placed it in the bed beside him. He covered it with the sheet, and lay awake in the hallway and listened.

### THREE

Bill Ledbetter hired the carpenter Guilford Nanney to build the
house for him in 1917, in the fork of a road, down the hill from
Rock Springs Baptist Church. The site is on an upland farm, on
the spine of a ridge ringed in the distance by mountains. The
house is white, surrounded on three sides by a porch. The steep
roof is covered with red tin, through which the upstairs dormer
windows peer out. The hallway is forty-one feet long, and just
over six feet wide. Its ceiling is nine feet two inches above the
floor. It bisects the house. Its walls and ceiling are unfinished
heart pine tongue-and-groove, red and dark now with age. The
walls are marked with hundreds of faint yellow streaks where for
years Paw-paw struck stick matches to light his cigarettes. The
streaks are curved upward at the ends, like fishhooks, where the

match sparked and Paw-paw lifted it away from the wall. The floor is made of four-inch pine boards, which were covered with carpet in 1978.

If you stand in the front door and look down the hallway to the back of the house, you will see on your left the doors to the living room, hall closet, dining room, and kitchen. On your right you will see two windows, the hall tree, the stairway curving up, the doors to the canning closet beneath the stairs and two bedrooms. My family knows the bedrooms as the front room and the back room. The doors, stair steps, banister, and railing are also unfinished pine. The doors have brass knobs; the railing is bright, and smooth enough to slide on. Three rooms are upstairs: the big room, the junk room, and Uncle Tom's room. My grandmother is displeased by the junk room. Early in their marriages her children asked her if they could store a few things upstairs that they did not have room for in their small, rented houses, and then never came back to get them.

FOUR

Before she married Bill Ledbetter, my great-grandmother was Sallie Ursula Edgerton. The Edgertons were granted a significant chunk of western North Carolina by an English king. Nobody remembers anymore exactly how much land, or even which king. It is doubtful that even the Edgertons at the time ever fully realized the extent of their holdings. They were rich as only people in a new world can be rich. They owned everything they could see. They owned the mountains in the distance. But generations passed. The Edgertons married local. There was no one else to marry. They gradually began to forget where they were from. They came to think of themselves as Carolinians, and then Americans, and then Confederates. They divided their land among themselves and among the mountain boys who married their daughters, and then divided it again. Over the course of two hundred years, North Carolina changed them from English aristocracy to country people with straight backs. Their dignity survived intact, but the family itself did not take a good hold. Their numbers did not improve over time, and their lot diminished. They began to die out.

FIVE

While we lived with Granny and Paw-paw, Mama put my playpen in the hallway, in the spot where Bill Ledbetter's bed used to be, so I could see out the front door. Paw-paw's beagles occasionally stopped at the screen and looked in. This made me laugh. Mama and Granny were busy with Shelly or napping for the next shift. They were not able to pay me much attention. I sat in the playpen, so the story goes, and looked at a *Reader's Digest*. I did not chew on it. I did not rip the pages out. I would not touch a *Progressive Farmer* or look at a *Life*. Do not ask me why. Once I fell asleep with a *Reader's Digest* covering my face. Paw-paw drove an old, green Lincoln. I could hear it coming up the ridge before anyone else. Mama and Granny say that every afternoon I announced his impending arrival by making a noise like a car.

## SIX

The last Edgerton to live on the Edgerton home place on Walnut Creek was my great-grandmother's uncle, Tom Edgerton. People said that Tom Edgerton wasn't right. He never married and lived alone in dignified, bewildered squalor. His dogs and chickens wandered in and out of the house. Some people believed he had a fortune squirreled away; his father had been known as Squire, and the Edgerton slaves were buried on the hill above the house. The way Tom Edgerton lived made the people who believed in the fortune angry. They tried to cheat him out of money. It felt to them like a right, a settling up. Tom Edgerton gave what little money he had away, and offered the people who came to cheat him sweet potatoes. He cooked the potatoes in the coals in the fireplace. His obliviousness and eccentricity embarrassed the few Edgertons who were left. By the end of his life, Tom Edgerton had to sleep in the crib to keep people from stealing his corn. After he died, people broke into his house and ripped down the wall boards and pried up the hearth stones. My great-grandmother inherited his farm. It became known as Bill Ledbetter's. My family refers to it as "down on the creek."

## SEVEN

By the time the sun came up, everyone in the house was afraid of the Bible salesman. The pacing had not stopped all night long.

Bill Ledbetter and my grandfather did not leave the house that morning to do their chores. Sallie Ledbetter and my grandmother herded my mother and Uncle Tom into the kitchen and ordered them to be quiet. When the Bible salesman came downstairs Bill Ledbetter offered him breakfast. Decorum would not permit him to do otherwise. My grandmother cooked eggs and grits and ham and biscuits as fast as she could. She cut up a cantaloupe but did not peel it.

Bill Ledbetter showed the Bible salesman a place at the dining-room table. Granny brought the food in from the kitchen. The Bible salesman ate with his fingers. He ate everything they heaped on his plate. He ate seconds and thirds. He ate all the biscuits in the basket and all the ham on the platter. He ate everything that was left on the table. My family was used to feeding field hands, men with large appetites who worked all day in the sun and maybe didn't have much food at home, but they had never seen anyone eat like the Bible salesman. He saved his cantaloupe slices for last. He ate the sweet meat, then he ate the rinds. Bill Ledbetter passed his cantaloupe rinds down the table. The Bible salesman ate them, too. When all the food was gone he stood and nodded and talked at them in strange words. He picked up his big suitcase and left the house and walked away up the ridge. My family watched him going up the road past the church until he was out of sight. They returned to the dining room and sat down around the table.

During the long night in his bed in the hallway, Bill Ledbetter had figured things out. The Bible salesman's suitcase had a false bottom. Beneath the false bottom the suitcase contained guns and bombs. The strange language he spoke was German.

Bill Ledbetter was angry at himself for not figuring things out sooner. My family sat around the dining-room table until far into the morning; the cows went without milking, the chickens without scratch. They gazed at the plate the Bible salesman had eaten from as if it were a relic. It was as clean as if a dog had licked it. They looked gratefully at one another. They did not say so, but were glad they had lived through the night.

EIGHT

Bill Ledbetter married up. Sallie Edgerton married well. Bill Ledbetter was a huge, strong man. In pictures his face is biblical and sharp, like Lincoln's. As a young man he watched the sun rise and set with the reins from his team of plow horses draped around his neck. The fields turned green and lush behind him. He started with nothing save prodigious strength and an unreasonable ambition, but was prosperous by the time he married Sallie Edgerton. He opened a general store. He bought a second farm, black bottomland on the Broad River. When his wife inherited Tom Edgerton's place he made the days long enough to work three farms at once. He hired field hands to help him, many of them black men named Edgerton. Lazy men could not work for Bill Ledbetter. He ran them off if they didn't quit first. When he hoed or picked cotton, he lapped everyone else in the field. He had water hauled to the hands in the rows so they would not waste time walking to the bucket.

One year he planted the largest bottom on the old Edgerton farm in head lettuce. People rode to the bottom from miles around to look at it. Few farmers then even grew lettuce in their gardens. Truck farming was unheard of. Sweet potatoes and small patches of tobacco were the only cash crops people thought to plant. Visitors to the bottom looked at the carefully hoed grid of lettuce hills stretching away toward the creek and snickered. They said Bill Ledbetter wouldn't be able to pay his help. But when the lettuce was ripe, Bill Ledbetter crated it up, stacked the crates into a tall, teetering load on the bed of his truck, and hauled it over the mountains to the farmer's market in Knoxville. He sold it for a dollar a head. People began to consider Bill Ledbetter's opinions carefully. Farmers planted head lettuce when he planted head lettuce and cucumbers when he planted cucumbers. He was elected to the school board. He taught himself to read music and led the singing at Rock Springs with a tuning fork. He traveled to Raleigh and told state legislators what was on his mind. In 1917 he hired Guilford Nanney to build him a house.

NINE

My cousins and I loved running up and down the hallway, but Paw-paw and Granny did not like for us to run inside the house. He was afraid we would fall and get hurt; she was afraid one of Paw-paw's guns would fall to the floor and discharge and kill us. Paw-paw kept shotguns and rifles hanging from the hat hooks on the hall tree, and from wire hooks high up on the wall. All of his guns stayed loaded. Paw-paw said there was no reason to keep a gun in the house if it wasn't loaded. Granny said there was no reason to keep a gun in the house if it was. This was one of the few points on which I ever heard them disagree.

Running up and down the hallway was one of the few ways we even considered disobeying Paw-paw and Granny. They were loath to spank us and rarely had to. We found the simple thought that one of them might be angry at us deterrent enough. But the hallway was our temptation, a fine line along the edge of their good graces. It was long enough to race in full speed. It demanded we run. Our feet pounding on the wooden floor thundered inside the tall, enclosed space. We became a herd, a posse. The brass doorknobs rattled as we passed. We made more noise when we ran than we absolutely had to. We made an altogether satisfactory racket.

Even under direct orders, a sideways look as we came in the front door was enough to propel the whole lot of us down the hallway. What happened then was always the same. Paw-paw rapped his knuckles against the living-room wall and said, "I'm gonna jerk a knot in somebody's tail," but by then we were pulling up at the opposite end of the house, where we met Granny coming out of the kitchen. She said, "You jaybirds stop all that running before one of those guns falls."

TEN

Guilford Nanney traveled the countryside building the tall houses he saw in his head. He was not a carpenter to whom you could present a plan drawn by someone else. You told him how many rooms you wanted, and he built you a house. That was the transaction. He would not suffer interference or meddling. The inordinate length of the hallway, the extravagant line and steep pitch of the roof were his idea alone. He lived in a small shack on the property, and started work mornings as soon as he could see. He sawed all of the framing for Bill Ledbetter's house and piled it in the front yard before he ever drove a nail. He did not use a blueprint, but when he put the house together, all the pieces fit. There were no studs or rafters or joists left over. He did not find this remarkable. The roof, seen from any angle, consists of a series of triangles, offset so that your eye is drawn upward as it is when you look at mountains and find yourself seeking the tallest peak. From the front door, the back door at the other end of the house seems as far away as the altar of a cathedral. The landing at the top of the stairs is cantilevered, and floats out over the hallway without betraying the intricacy of the structure that supports it or the complexity of thought behind it.

## ELEVEN

My cousins and sister ran barefoot up and down the hallway in the summer, but often pulled up lame and crying, with long, jagged splinters impaled in the bottoms of their feet. Granny rounded up the injured cousin and sat them down in a straight chair in the kitchen. She dug at the splinter with a needle sterilized in alcohol. The cousin screamed and flapped their arms; Granny threatened and scolded and cajoled. She swore that in just a minute she was going to pop somebody if the racket didn't stop; she said she would get a switch after the whole lot of us if we didn't get out of her light so she could see.

When the splinter came loose she presented it to the sobbing cousin for inspection. She applied red Mercurochrome, which didn't burn, or orange Merthiolate, which did, to the wound. We all sucked in our breath and watched the cousin's face when it was Merthiolate. The cousin limped down the hallway with the needle to show the splinter to Paw-paw. The rest of us followed along behind, grumbling by then at the cousin's hysteria. Paw-paw took the cousin up into his lap and patted them on the leg and pretended not to be able to see the splinter, it was so small. He looked carefully at the red or orange stain on the bottom of the cousin's foot and said that he thought it was going to be all right. The rest of us gathered around Paw-paw's chair and leaned toward him. He smelled like aftershave and Vitalis. Each of us secretly wished we had been fortunate enough to have been injured so grievously.

## TWELVE

It is said that as Bill Ledbetter watched the tall, skeletal peaks of his new roof rising, he was sickened by the amount of lumber Guilford Nanney used. Bill Ledbetter was not by nature an extravagant man. He wanted a big house, but could not sanction waste. While it is unknown whether he said anything to Guilford Nanney about what he considered gratuitous use of material, it is known that Guilford Nanney left the job suddenly while there was still trim work to be done around the doors and windows upstairs. He took a job building the first set of steps to the top of Chimney Rock, a mountain visible from Bill Ledbetter's front yard. Rich men were making the mountain into a park. No one knows if Bill Ledbetter complained about Guilford Nanny's desertion. He simply finished the house himself. While Bill Ledbetter's carpentry work is level and adequate and square, it is not hard to spot. The only hammer marks in the whole house belong to Bill Ledbetter. It is easy to tell at the top of the stairs where one man left a job, and another man took it up.

### THIRTEEN

Sallie Ledbetter was never a robust woman and did not bear children easily. The first child she had with Bill Ledbetter was a girl, Clydie Belle. Clydie was frail from the time of her birth and did not live to see a healthy day. She died of colitis when she was seven months old. Their second child, a son, was born prematurely and lived only an hour. They did not name him. My grandfather, William Dan, was their third and last child. As a baby he was small and sickly and Sallie Ledbetter feared for his health. She kept him in her bed to keep him warm. She was afraid Bill Ledbetter would turn over in his sleep on the baby, so she banished him to another bed.

When Bill Ledbetter moved his family into the new house Guilford Nanney built, he put his bed in the hallway and slept there for the next thirty years. My grandfather slept in the front room in the bed with his mother until he was a tall and gangly boy. When Bill Ledbetter finally made Paw-paw move to another room, Sallie Ledbetter did not ask him to return to her bed, or perhaps by then he did not want to go. My family is unsure how this part of the story goes. Bill Ledbetter did not sleep again in the same room with his wife until 1947, when he was an old man sick with lung cancer. He had his bed moved to the front room from the hallway because in his illness he could no longer keep warm.


### FOURTEEN


*My story goes like this:* I jerked the front screen door open and ran as hard as I could. The house was Fenway Park in Boston, the hallway the first-base path. The door swinging shut behind me was a throw whizzing in from short. If I hit the back door before the front door slammed, I was safe. If the front door slammed first, I was out. I hit the back screen running and crossed the porch in a step and jumped off into the yard and kept going. I went for extra bases. The game then became problematic, a matter of judgment and honesty. The spring on the back door was pulling it closed. The clothesline pole was too close, too easy to reach in time, to be an acceptable base; the woodshed was too far away. There was no quantitative way to make the call of safe or out. I had to decide when the door slammed where I was on the field. Sometimes I slowed up with a single, disappointed skip and slapped my hands on my thighs and turned toward the dugout. I was out. Sometimes I clapped my hands once and reached out to accept the congratulatory handshake of an imaginary teammate. *Earley scores. He has good speed. He's having a heck of a year.* In my mind's eye, I was always on television. I interviewed myself in the woodshed, where no one could see me from the house. I took off my cap and wiped my brow with the back of my arm.

I spoke into a piece of kindling. I said, "Thanks. I felt good today. I'm just glad I could help the team."

## FIFTEEN

A corner cupboard from the Edgerton home place used to sit in the dining room. It was built by Edgerton slaves out of wide oak boards. It was big and dark and solid as a vault. When I was a little kid I had to stand on a chair to see what was inside it. Paw-paw stored his tools on the top three shelves. Behind the wide doors he kept dark, heavy wrenches and hammers and screwdrivers and files, and old coffee cans filled with nuts and bolts and screws and the occasional odd shotgun shell. There were leftover balls of baling twine, and twisted leather gloves fragrant with grease, and inscrutable pieces of machinery, parts of tractors and balers and combines and trucks; there were chains and spare tines from cultivators and planters and plows. Granny kept tablecloths and towels and napkins and washcloths on the bottom two shelves. The cupboard smelled like washing powder and clean cotton, stiffened by the sun, like rust and leather and creosote. It smelled like a warm barn and fresh sheets.

Paw-paw showed the cupboard once to an antiques dealer. The man wanted immediately to buy it. He tried to buy it for years. Paw-paw did not sell it until 1978, after he was sick, when the house had begun to seem big and cold. The antiques dealer gave five hundred dollars for the cupboard. Paw-paw and Granny used the money to carpet the hallway. Granny says today that she does not wish the cupboard back, even though it would be worth thousands of dollars. She says the only furniture she's ever known was dark and ponderous and ugly to look at. Much of it came from the Edgertons and was old already when she married Dan Ledbetter in 1933 and moved into the house. She does not understand the modern Southern passion for antiques. She would not walk to the mailbox for a truckload. She wanted her whole life to get rid of old things, and replace them with new. She especially does not miss sweeping the hallway. Forty-five years was long enough. She memorized the grain in the flooring. She wore out more brooms than she cares to remember. She still considers the cupboard for the carpet a good trade.

## SIXTEEN

*And this:* Granny and Paw-paw slept in the front room. Paw-paw kept a loaded .38 revolver in a cigar box in the nightstand by the bed. On Sundays after church I used to sneak down the hallway into their room to look at it. It was a black, antique Smith & Wesson. I was strictly forbidden to touch it. One Sunday I pulled the hammer back and cocked it. At that moment I felt the gun become a living thing in my hand. It felt as dangerous as a coiled snake. I was afraid to breathe. I was nine or ten years old. I didn't know what to do. I couldn't call for help because I would get into trouble; I couldn't put it back in the cigar box because it was cocked.

I was afraid to uncock the gun because it might fire. I had seen people uncock guns on television hundreds of times. They held the hammer back with a thumb and pulled the trigger, but they were Marshal Dillon and Mannix and McGarrett and Gil Favor. If the hammer slipped from beneath my thumb the gun would go off. It would kill me or shoot through one of the walls. I became conscious of where my family was in the house. Mama and Granny were in the kitchen cooking dinner. Daddy was in the living room reading and Paw-paw was sitting on the front porch with his feet on the railing. I didn't know where Shelly was. There seemed to be no safe place to point the gun. I was sure I was going to kill someone, and the fear I felt turned also into a kind of sadness, an anticipation of loss. I moaned out loud, although I did not want or mean to. I prayed for God to help me. I gasped and closed my eyes and gripped the hammer with both thumbs and pulled the trigger. The gun did not fire. The hammer came loose beneath my thumbs and I held it poised for a moment above the firing pin. Then I lowered it slowly. The gun returned to sleep in my hand. I placed it back in the cigar box. I put the cigar box back in the nightstand. I wiped my hands on my pants and backed into the hallway. I ran down the hallway hard as I could and through the back door and across the porch and jumped off into the yard. I was almost to the woodshed before the back door slammed.

SEVENTEEN

It is a credit to my grandmother that to this day she will not speak ill of Sallie Ledbetter. Granny's maiden name was Clara Mae Womack. She grew up on a small farm where Walnut Creek empties into the Green River, several miles below Tom Edgerton's place. She married Dan Ledbetter in 1933, when she was nineteen years old. He was twenty-eight. She did not kiss him until after they were engaged, and then she put a chair between them so he couldn't get his arms around her. They had planned to live in the small house the Ledbetters had lived in before the big house was built, but Sallie Ledbetter forbade her son to move out. Later she had the older house torn down to keep him at home.

While the big house with the red roof was known as Bill Ledbetter's place, it was Sallie Ledbetter who decreed what was what inside it. When Clara Mae Ledbetter moved in, Sallie Ledbetter stopped cooking altogether. Granny cooked breakfast before dawn, a big dinner for the field hands at noon, and supper for the family in the evening. She did most of the cleaning and washing. Her life was not easy. If she and Paw-paw went upstairs together during the day, Sallie Ledbetter called her daughter-in-law back downstairs because it did not look proper. She scolded the two of them if they went for a walk alone.

When my uncle Tom was born, Sallie Ledbetter insisted the baby sleep with her. The room Paw-paw and Granny slept in did not have a stove, and Sallie Ledbetter said the baby would get sick in the cold. She did not express the same concern later for my mother and my aunt Barbara, who slept in unheated rooms from the time they were born until they married and moved away. Uncle Tom slept with Sallie Ledbetter until he was a tall and gangly boy. She would not let him eat watermelon because she thought watermelon had given Clydie colitis. Granny could not put her foot down because it was not her house, and Paw-paw would not stand up to his mother. Bill Ledbetter had no interest in the affairs of women. Inside the house Sallie Ledbetter's every wish was set in stone. Granny had nowhere to turn. She could not run the house the way she saw fit until Sallie Edgerton Ledbetter died in 1953. Sallie Ledbetter also died of lung cancer, although neither she nor Bill Ledbetter had ever smoked.

## EIGHTEEN

I chased my cousin Janet up the front steps. She squealed and opened the front door and ran into the house. We started down the hallway at a dead run. The screen door slammed behind us. A double-barreled twenty-gauge shotgun slipped from the top row of hat hooks on the hall tree and fell and clattered onto the floor. Janet and I stopped in our tracks. We tiptoed back down the hallway and stared at the shotgun. It hadn't fired.

Paw-paw ran from the living room. Granny came down the hallway at a gallop from the kitchen. The falling gun had split the hall tree seat in two. Janet and I were terrified. We said that we hadn't done it, that we were just running down the hallway and the gun fell. Paw-paw's face flushed red. He began to shake. We had never seen him that angry. His fists were clenched at his sides. We could tell he didn't know what to do next. Janet and I held our breath as if waiting for an explosion.

"Damn," Paw-paw said.

"Dan!" Granny said. Paw-paw didn't believe in cursing.

"Damn, damn, damn, damn, damn," Paw-paw said. He seemed to like it, now that he had started. He unbuckled his belt. He had never whipped any of us before. Granny did all the spanking, and she popped us so lightly that sometimes it was hard not to laugh. Paw-paw jerked his belt out through the loops. Janet and I began to cry. Paw-paw was tall as a giant. "How many times have I told you not to run in this house?" he said.

"Please don't whip us, Paw-paw," we said.

"Dan Ledbetter," Granny said, "you're not going to whip anybody. You're lucky that gun didn't go off. I've told you and told you not to keep those guns loaded."

Paw-paw and Granny stared at each other and went out the front door and down the steps and around the side of the house. Janet and I tiptoed into the living room and peeked out the window. We could see them arguing through the gap between the two heating oil tanks at the side of the house, but the window was closed and we couldn't hear what they said. We had never seen them argue before and it scared us to watch. Paw-paw still held his belt in his hand. Janet thought they were going to get a divorce.

Paw-paw pointed at the house and said something angry to Granny. We could tell he was talking about us. Granny pointed at the house and said something angry back. She was talking about him. Paw-paw spun away from her and walked away. We ran to the window on the other side of the room to see where he went. He walked quickly across the front yard and got in his car and drove away. Granny came back in and ordered me into the back room and Janet to the front room. She told us that if she heard a sound out of either of us she would get a switch after us, and we could tell she meant what she said. I don't know about Janet, but I cried into the pillow on the bed in the back room. I was sure Paw-paw hated me.

## NINETEEN

Dan Ledbetter grew to be as tall as Bill Ledbetter, but did not inherit his father's strength or stamina. He was six feet four, but so skinny that he seemed to have been constructed from spare parts. In photographs his legs seem much too long and delicate, the rest of his body ill supported, dangerously high above the ground. Only near the end of his life, when he grew a small, incongruous potbelly, did he ever weigh more than one hundred and fifty pounds. He wore only long-sleeved shirts, whose cuffs he kept tightly buttoned at the wrist. And if he suffered in physical comparison with Bill Ledbetter, Paw-paw fared no better in comparisons of accomplishment. Even on a tractor, he could never do in a day the work his father did in the same amount of time with a team of horses. The sun never stood still above the fields in which he worked.

That people looked to Dan Ledbetter to match his father in word and deed, when he was incapable of doing so, was perhaps my grandfather's heaviest burden. Bill Ledbetter delighted in firing both barrels of his massive English 10-gauge shotgun at once, while Paw-paw found shooting the gun a barrel at a time as unpleasant as any other ordinary man would have. The one time Paw-paw fired both barrels simultaneously, the recoil turned him around in his tracks. He never planted a cash crop for which there was a demand a year before there was a supply. He never had an opinion he considered worthy of taking to Raleigh to share with a state legislator. He never bought land or led the singing in church. He spent his life presiding over the slow dissipation of Bill Ledbetter's immaculate farms. Through no fault of his own he became the measuring stick people used to construct Bill Ledbetter's legend. That legend was in turn used to measure him.

## TWENTY

After a while Paw-paw blew the horn in the front yard. Janet and I opened the doors and looked tentatively out into the hallway. Granny came out of the kitchen with Paw-paw's cap and a plastic margarine dish filled with food scraps from dinner. Every day Paw-paw rode down to the creek to feed the cows. It was a favorite expedition among the cousins. He always took scraps for the cats who lived in the barn. The cats rubbed against his legs, but ran away when we tried to touch them. Granny motioned for us to follow her and walked down the hallway and held the screen door open. She handed me Paw-paw's cap and the scraps for the cats. Paw-paw didn't like to go anywhere without his cap. He had left the house without it earlier. "Go on out there," she said. "He's not mad at you."

Janet and I went slowly down the front steps and walked across the yard toward the car. The motor was running. Paw-paw watched us through the windshield. We walked up close to the car and stopped. I couldn't tell if he was mad or not. I was afraid to say anything. I handed him his cap. He said, "You knotheads going with me?"

We ran around the car and opened the door and climbed in.

Janet slid up close beside Paw-paw. I rolled down the window. On the way to the creek Paw-paw stopped at Eddy Bailey's store and bought us each a Mountain Dew and a pack of M&M's. He did not mention the hall tree, then or ever. He had a carpenter glue the two halves of the seat back together. If you examine the seat today, you cannot tell it was ever broken.

## TWENTY-ONE

Bill Ledbetter's strength was an act of nature: random and unique, indifferent and cruel as a storm. He lived in solitude inside his great body. He did not understand weakness because he had never known it; he was oblivious as a tree to the straining inside the lesser bodies around him. When he stood at the front of Rock Springs Baptist Church on Sunday mornings and tapped his tuning fork on the Communion table and held it to his ear, it seemed to him proper that only he could hear the note. For that reason he prevented the church from buying a piano as long as he lived.

After Sunday dinner Bill Ledbetter sat in the shade on the corner of the porch and with the tuning fork sang his way through one of the Baptist hymnals he ordered from all over the country. The fields bloomed all around him while he sang. He offered the hymns as thanks to God. His family gathered around him and listened, but only listened; he did not ask them to join him. He was a man of great faith, but his understanding of God revolved only around the work he could do himself between dawn and dark, six days a week, and the countable ways that work was rewarded. It did not occur to him that other men might strike their own deals with God in different currencies. He never thought to teach his only son the things he had learned.

Bill Ledbetter made no provision for his family after his passing, other than leaving them the land he had accumulated over the years. He did not believe in insurance. When his general store burned down years before, he had not been able to replace it. He died in 1947 after a long stay at Baptist Hospital in Winston-Salem. My family found itself land rich, but cash poor. Paw-paw had to sell the farm on the river to pay Bill Ledbetter's medical bills. That first spring, he had to hire someone to lay out the corn rows in the remaining Ledbetter bottoms because he did not know how. He was forty-two years old, and had farmed his entire life, but his father had never trusted him with anything important. Bill Ledbetter had reserved for himself the labors that required thought or skill. The fields Paw-paw planted in sweet potatoes that year came up in Johnson grass and did not make a crop.

## TWENTY-TWO

For years I tried to jump high enough to touch the ceiling in the hallway. I never came close until the Sunday my middle finger brushed the wood. In the slow movement of time as it is measured by children, I had been trying to touch the ceiling forever. I was fourteen years old, and could not believe I had finally done it. I jumped again to verify what had happened, and again my middle finger brushed the dark pine. I had crossed some threshold I couldn't name, but felt a profound, if equally nameless, pleasure at finding myself on the other side. One Sunday I couldn't jump high enough to touch a ceiling nine feet two inches above the floor, but the next Sunday I could. This simple fact came to stand during my adolescence as a constant, quantifiable measurement of *something*. I checked it every Sunday the way a meteorologist might check gauges. That I could always touch the ceiling when I jumped provided a small, welcome comfort, a marking of joy, like the continued existence of weather.

Soon I could touch the ceiling with increasingly larger portions of my hand: two fingers, then three fingers, then four. By the time my sister Shelly died in December 1979, of injuries she received in a car accident, I could jump high enough to place both palms flat against the ceiling. I checked this measurement immediately after her funeral, still wearing my suit and dress shoes.

After Shelly died I continued jumping in the hallway, but came to view the fact that I could still slap my hands on the ceiling as verification of nothing so much as God's unfairness. I wanted to know why Shelly had died and I had lived; I became so adamant in the face of the unanswerable that my life unraveled around the question. Shelly's lifelong anger not only filled me with regret at the times I had deserved to be its object, but with certainty that it had been a premonition she had not been able to voice. I hadn't understood what she was trying to say until it was too late to make amends. Although we no doubt loved each other, we never really got along. It seemed to me then, and in the secret part of my heart where I hold unreasonable truths seems to me still, that Shelly came into this world knowing she would not be here long. She spent her short life in a howl of protest untranslatable by the people she loved most.

I also came to believe that I was somehow beneficiary of Shelly's death, that an account had been settled in my favor. I began to think I was invincible. I thought I would live forever. My jumping took on a desperate, daredevil quality. In the woods behind Granny's house I jumped over the chest-high barbed wire  fence that separated her property from that of a neighbor. I took running starts and leaped over picnic tables and shrubs, and once over a parked MG Midget. I stood flat-footed and vaulted over chairs, trash cans, lengthwise over coffee tables, up four, five, six steps of my dormitory stairwell. What I did not take into account when jumping was the accumulated violence of landing. I jumped as if my immortality had been bought and paid for, without realizing that each time my feet hit the ground I paid a corresponding physical price. Eventually, my knees and ankles began to give out. By the time I was twenty-five, I was hesitant to jump over the net on a tennis court, a leap I would have considered paltry a few years before. I was afraid of how much it would hurt when I landed.

As I write this, I am thirty-three years old, and no longer jump well at all. On a good day I can touch the hallway ceiling with my three longest fingers. Although I didn't realize it at the time, the thing I began measuring with that first jump nineteen years ago was the inevitable arc of my own mortality. The day is approaching fast when I won't be able to touch the ceiling at all. And while I realize the vanity and uselessness and ingratitude inherent in any evaluation of self-worth based solely on accomplishment of the body, it is still a day I dread. I am sensitive to the power of metaphor to the point of superstition. It was metaphor that frightened Bill Ledbetter the first morning the cancer sprouting in his lungs prevented him for the first time in his life from going to the fields and doing a day's work. Metaphor was the stranger outside in the dark from whom my grandfather sought to protect himself with the shotguns and rifles that lined the hallway, and metaphor that rode as a friend in his left breast pocket until it finally killed him. It was metaphor that left sulfurous tracks on the walls of the hallway you can still see today. The last five years of his life Paw-paw had to sleep sitting up in order to catch his breath. While I cannot recall the sound of his voice, I can still hear him cough. It was metaphor that kept us all awake and listening during those nights. We were all afraid Paw-paw was going to die, and eventually he did, six months after we buried Shelly. The metaphors of his life hardened into facts.

That I can't remember a single thing my sister said to me is a fact.

That Granny is eighty years old is a fact.

I wish that with these words I could turn the hallway into perfect metaphor, an incantation that would restore everyone who ever walked its length to the person they wanted most in their best heart to be, but the fact is that the hallway is simply a space forty-one feet long, nine feet two inches high, and just over six feet wide, through which my family has traveled for seventy-eight years. Of all the facts we have gathered and stored in the hallway, this one troubles me most: stories in real life rarely end the way we want them to. They simply end.

## HENRY LOUIS GATES, JR.

When I was growing up in Piedmont, West Virginia, the TV was the ritual arena for the drama of race. In our family, it was located in the living room, where it functioned like a fireplace in the proverbial New England winter. I'd sit in the water in the galvanized tub in the middle of our kitchen, watching the TV in the next room while Mama did the laundry or some other chore as she waited for Daddy to come home from his second job. We watched people getting hosed and cracked over their heads, people being spat upon and arrested, rednecks siccing fierce dogs on women and children, our people responding by singing and marching and staying strong. Eyes on the prize. Eyes on the prize. George Wallace at the gate of the University of Alabama, blocking Autherine Lucy's way. Charlayne Hunter at the University of Georgia. President Kennedy interrupting our scheduled program with a special address, saying that James Meredith will *definitely* enter the University of Mississippi; and saying it like he believed it (unlike Ike), saying it like the big kids said "It's our turn to play" on the basketball court and walking all through us as if we weren't there.

The simple truth is that the civil rights era came late to Piedmont, even though it came early to our television set. We could watch what was going on Elsewhere on television, but the marches and sit-ins were as remote to us as, in other ways, was the all-colored world of *Amos and Andy*—a world full of black lawyers, black judges, black nurses, black doctors.

Politics aside, though, we were starved for images of ourselves and searched TV to find them. Everybody, of course, watched sports, because Piedmont was a big sports town. Making the big leagues was like getting to heaven, and everybody had hopes that they could, or a relative could. We'd watch the games day and night, and listen on radio to what we couldn't see. Everybody knew the latest scores, batting averages, rbi's, and stolen bases. Everybody knew the standings in the leagues, who could still win the pennant and how. Everybody liked the Dodgers because of Jackie Robinson, the same way everybody still voted Republican because of Abraham Lincoln. Sports on the mind, sports in the mind. The only thing to rival the Valley in fascination was the big-league baseball diamond.

I once heard Mr. James Helms say, "You got to give the white man his due when it comes to technology. One on one, though, and it's even-steven. Joe Louis showed 'em that." We were obsessed with sports in part because it was the only time we could compete with white people even-steven. And the white people, it often seemed, were just as obsessed with this primal confrontation between the races as we were. I think they integrated professional sports, after all those years of segregation, just to capitalize on this voyeuristic thrill of the forbidden contact. What interracial sex was to the seventies, interracial sports were to the fifties. Except for sports, we rarely saw a colored person on TV.

Actually, I first got to know white people as "people" through their flickering images on television shows. It was the television set that brought us together at night, and the television set that brought in the world outside the Valley. We were close enough to Washington to receive its twelve channels on cable. Piedmont was transformed from a radio culture to one with the fullest range of television, literally overnight. During my first-grade year, we'd watch *Superman, Lassie,* Jack Benny, Danny Thomas, *Robin Hood, I Love Lucy, December Bride,* Nat King Cole (of course), *Wyatt Earp, Broken Arrow,* Phil Silvers, Red Skelton, *The $64,000 Question, Ozzie and Harriet, The Millionaire, Father Knows Best, The Lone Ranger,* Bob Cummings, *Dragnet, The People's Choice, Rin Tin Tin, Jim Bowie, Gunsmoke, My Friend Flicka, The Life of Riley, Topper, Dick Powell's Zane Grey Theater, Circus Boy,* and Loretta Young—all in prime time. My favorites were *The Life of Riley,* in part because he worked in a factory like Daddy did, and *Ozzie and Harriet,* in part because Ozzie never seemed to work at all. A year later, however, *Leave It to Beaver* swept most of the others away.

With a show like *Topper,* I felt as if I was getting a glimpse, at last, of the life that Mrs. Hudson, and Mrs. Thomas, and Mrs. Campbell must be leading in their big mansions on East Hampshire Street. Smoking jackets and cravats, spats and canes, elegant garden parties and martinis. People who wore suits to eat dinner!

This was a world so elegantly distant from ours, it was like a voyage to another galaxy, light-years away.

*Leave It to Beaver,* on the other hand, was a world much closer, but just out of reach nonetheless. Beaver's street was where we wanted to live, Beaver's house where we wanted to eat and sleep, Beaver's father's firm where we'd have liked Daddy to work. These shows for us were about property, the property that white people could own and that we couldn't. About a level of comfort and ease at which we could only wonder. It was the world that the integrated school was going to prepare us to enter and that, for Mama, would be the prize.

If prime time consisted of images of middle-class white people who looked nothing at all like us, late night was about the radio, listening to *Randy's Record Shop* from Gallatin, Tennessee. My brother, Rocky, kept a transistor radio by his bed, and he'd listen to it all night, for all I knew, long after I'd fallen asleep. In 1956, black music hadn't yet broken down into its many subgenres, except for large divisions such as jazz, blues, gospel, rhythm and blues. On *Randy's,* you were as likely to hear The Platters doing "The Great Pretender" and Clyde McPhatter doing "Treasure of Love" as you were to hear Howlin' Wolf do "Smokestack Lightning" or Joe Turner do "Corrine, Corrine." My own favorite that year was the slow, deliberate sound of Jesse Belvin's "Goodnight, My Love." I used to fall asleep singing it in my mind to my Uncle Earkie's girlfriend Ula, who was a sweet caffè latte brown, with the blackest, shiniest straight hair and the fullest, most rounded red lips. Not even in your dreams, he had said to me one day, as I watched her red dress slink down our front stairs. It was my first brush with the sublime.

We used to laugh at the way the disc jockey sang "Black

Strap Lax-a-teeves" during the commercials. I sometimes would wonder if the kids we'd seen on TV in Little Rock or Birmingham earlier in the evening were singing themselves to sleep with *their* Ulas.

Lord knows, we weren't going to learn how to be colored by watching television. Seeing somebody colored on TV was an event.

"Colored, colored, on Channel Two," you'd hear someone shout. Somebody else would run to the phone, while yet another hit the front porch, telling all the neighbors where to see it. And *everybody* loved *Amos and Andy*—I don't care what people say today. For the colored people, the day they took *Amos and Andy* off the air was one of the saddest days in Piedmont, about as sad as the day of the last mill pic-a-nic.

What was special to us about *Amos and Andy* was that their world was *all* colored, just like ours. Of course, *they* had their colored judges and lawyers and doctors and nurses, which we could only dream about having, or becoming—and we *did* dream about those things. Kingfish ate his soft-boiled eggs delicately, out of an egg cup. He even owned an acre of land in Westchester County, which he sold to Andy, using the facade of a movie set to fake a mansion. As far as we were concerned, the foibles of Kingfish or Calhoun the lawyer were the foibles of individuals who happened to be funny. Nobody was likely to confuse them with the colored people we knew, no more than we'd confuse ourselves with the entertainers and athletes we saw on TV or in *Ebony* or *Jet,* the magazines we devoured to keep up with what was happening with the race. And people took special relish in Kingfish's malapropisms. "I denies the allegation, Your Honor, and I resents the alligator."

In one of my favorite episodes of *Amos and Andy*, "The Punjab of Java-Pour," Andy Brown is hired to advertise a brand of coffee and is required to dress up as a turbaned Oriental potentate. Kingfish gets the bright idea that if he dresses up as a potentate's servant, the two of them can enjoy a vacation at a luxury hotel for free. So attired, the two promenade around the lobby, running up an enormous tab and generously dispensing "rubies" and "diamonds" as tips. The plan goes awry when people try to redeem the gems and discover them to be colored glass. It was widely suspected that this episode was what prompted two Negroes in Baltimore to dress like African princes and demand service in a segregated four-star restaurant. Once it was clear to the management that these were not American Negroes, the two were treated royally. When the two left the restaurant, they took off their African headdresses and robes and enjoyed a hearty laugh at the restaurant's expense. "They weren't like our Negroes," the maître d' told the press in explaining why he had agreed to seat the two "African princes."

Whenever the movies *Imitation of Life* and *The Green Pastures* would be shown on TV, we watched with similar hunger—especially *Imitation of Life.* It was never on early; only the late *late* show, like the performances of Cab Calloway and Duke Ellington at the Crystal Palace. And we'd stay up. Everybody colored. The men coming home on second shift from the paper mill would stay up. Those who had to go out on the day shift and who normally would have been in bed hours earlier (because they had to be at work at 6:30) would stay up. As would we, the kids, wired for the ritual at hand. And we'd all sit in silence, fighting back the tears, watching as Delilah invents the world's greatest pancakes and a down-and-out Ned Sparks takes one taste and says, flatly, "We'll box it." Cut to a big white house, plenty of money, and Delilah saying that she doesn't want her share of the money (which should have been *all* the money); she just wants to continue to cook, clean, wash, iron, and serve her good white lady and her daughter. (Nobody in our living room was going for *that*.) And then Delilah shows up at her light-complected daughter's school one day, unexpectedly, to pick her up, and there's the daughter, Peola, ducking down behind her books, and the white teacher saying, I'm sorry, ma'am, there must be some mistake. We have no little colored children here. And then Delilah, spying her baby, says, Oh, yes you do. Peola! Peola! Come here to your mammy, honey chile. And then Peola runs out of the room, breaking her poor, sweet mother's heart. And Peola continues to break her mother's heart, by passing, leaving the race, and marrying white. Yet her mama understands, always understands, and, dying, makes detailed plans for her own big, beautiful funeral, complete with six white horses and a carriage and a jazz band, New Orleans style. And she dies and is about to be buried, when, out of nowhere, comes grown-up Peola, saying, "Don't die, Mama, don't die, Mama, I'm sorry, Mama, I'm sorry," and throws her light-and-bright-and-damn-near-white self onto her mama's casket. By this time, we have stopped trying to fight back the tears and are boo-hooing all over the place. Then we turn to our *own* mama and tell her how much we love her and swear that we will *never, ever* pass for white. I promise, Mama. I promise.

Peola had sold her soul to the Devil. This was the first popular Faust in the black tradition, the bargain with the Devil over the cultural soul. Talk about a cautionary tale.

*The Green Pastures* was an altogether more uplifting view of things, our Afro Paradiso. Make way for the Lawd! Make way for the Lawd! And Rex Ingram, dressed in a long black frock coat and a long white beard, comes walking down the Streets Paved with Gold, past the Pearly Gates, while Negroes with the whitest wings of fluffy cotton fly around heaven, playing harps, singing spirituals, having fish fries, and eating watermelon. Hard as I try, I can't stop seeing God as that black man who played Him in *The Green Pastures* and seeing Noah as Rochester from the Jack Benny show, trying to bargain with God to let him take along an extra keg of wine or two.

Civil rights took us all by surprise. Every night we'd wait until the news to see what "Dr. King and dem" were doing. It was like watching the Olympics or the World Series when somebody colored was on. The murder of Emmett Till was one of my first memories. He whistled at some white girl, they said; that's all he did. He was beat so bad they didn't even want to open the casket, but his mama made them. She wanted the world to see what they had done to her baby.

In 1957, when I was in second grade, black children integrated Central High School in Little Rock, Arkansas. We watched it on TV. All of us watched it. I don't mean Mama and Daddy and Rocky. I mean *all* the colored people in America watched it, together, with one set of eyes. We'd watch it in the morning, on the *Today* show on NBC, before we'd go to school; we'd watch it in the evening, on the news, with Edward R. Murrow on CBS. We'd watch the Special Bulletins at night, interrupting our TV shows.

The children were all well scrubbed and greased down, as

we'd say. Hair short and closely cropped, parted, and oiled (the boys); "done" in a "permanent" and straightened, with turned-up bangs and curls (the girls). Starched shirts, white, and creased pants, shoes shining like a buck private's spit shine. Those Negroes were *clean*. The fact was, those children trying to get the right to enter that school in Little Rock looked like black versions of models out of *Jack & Jill* magazine, to which my mama had subscribed for me so that I could see what children outside the Valley were up to. "They hand-picked those children," Daddy would say. "No dummies, no nappy hair, heads not too kinky, lips not too thick, no disses and no dats." At seven, I was dismayed by his cynicism. It bothered me somehow that those children would have been chosen, rather than just having shown up or volunteered or been nearby in the neighborhood.

Daddy was jaundiced about the civil rights movement, and especially about the Reverend Dr. Martin Luther King, Jr. He'd say all of his names, to drag out his scorn. By the mid-sixties, we'd argue about King from sunup to sundown. Sometimes he'd just mention King to get a rise from me, to make a sagging evening more interesting, to see if I had *learned* anything real yet, to see how long I could think up counter arguments before getting so mad that my face would turn purple. I think he just liked the color purple on my face, liked producing it there. But he was not of two minds about those children in Little Rock.

The children would get off their school bus surrounded by soldiers from the National Guard and by a field of state police. They would stop at the steps of the bus and seem to take a very deep breath. Then the phalanx would start to move slowly along this gulley of sidewalk and rednecks that connected the steps of the school bus with the white wooden double doors of the school. All kinds of crackers would be lining that gulley, separated from the phalanx of children by rows of state police, who formed a barrier arm in arm. Cheerleaders from the all-white high school that was desperately trying to stay that way were dressed in those funny little pleated skirts, with a big red *C* for "Central" on their chests, and they'd wave their pom-poms and start to cheer: "Two, four, six, eight—We don't want to integrate!" And all those crackers and all those rednecks would join in that chant as if their lives depended on it. Deafening, it was: even on our twelve-inch TV, a three-inch speaker buried along the back of its left side.

Whatever tumult our small screen revealed, though, the dawn of the civil rights era could be no more than a spectator sport from our living room in Piedmont. It was almost like a war being fought overseas. And all things considered, white and colored Piedmont got along pretty well in those years, the fifties and early sixties. At least as long as colored people didn't try to sit down in the Cut-Rate or at the Rendezvous Bar, or eat pizza at Eddie's, or buy property, or move into the white neighborhoods, or dance with, date, or dilate upon white people. Not to mention try to get a job in the craft unions at the paper mill. Or have a drink at the white VFW, or join the white American Legion, or get loans at the bank, or just generally get out of line. Other than that, colored and white got on pretty well.

## KAREN KARBO

You live with your parents in an apartment building called The Something Arms in Sherman Oaks, a sun-blasted suburb of Los Angeles. The building is standard Sun Belt issue, white stucco flecked with gold, a rectangular swimming pool with no diving board, a panel of mailboxes just inside the front gate. You live in an upstairs apartment overlooking the Dumpsters. Your dining-room table is a card table, your dining room is the kitchen side of the living room. They are just starting out, your parents. It is 1962.

Every stuffy apartment has a kid or two in it. All you need to go swimming is one adult sitting poolside. It is usually a mother. It is usually your mother, who can't swim herself, who is allergic to the sun, but has an itch, always, to be out of the apartment. She is a woman with itches, your mother. Days before she dies she will admit as much. She will tell you she was born in the wrong time. She will tell you she should have been you.

One afternoon, when you are five or six, you are showing your mother how you can swim the entire length of the pool without coming up for air. Your mother is sitting on a chaise, drinking beer and clipping articles about decorating from *Family Circle*. You go under and she is watching you from over the rim of her glass. When you come up you find her talking to Bernie, the mailman. She is making him laugh with a story about how, in her high school Senior Will, she bequeathed her thick copper-colored hair to every girl in the school. How she got on to this subject, you will never know. It is part of what your mother calls the Gift of Gab, something, along with your mother's fine hair, you failed to inherit.

The dining-room table, the card table, is the only table in the apartment. Your mother sews at this table, hemming large squares of floral fabric in the earth tones of the era—brown, gold, avocado—tablecloths for this very table. You learn cursive writing at this table, your pencil marks pocked and wobbly from writing on the squishy vinyl surface.

At parent-teacher conferences Mrs. Warnack, your first-grade teacher, tells your mother that your writing resembles the hand of Mrs. Warnack's maiden aunt.

You ask your mother, What's maiden? Your mother says it's what happens when a girl winds up old and unloved.

Mrs. Warnack also tells your mother that while she enjoys having you in class, you need to learn self-control.

You ask your mother, What's self-control? Your mother says not having it is how a girl winds up old and unloved.

When your parents have saved up enough for a down payment, they move to a house in the suburbs, a tract house on the border of Whittier and La Habra, also the border of Los Angeles County and Orange County.

One side of the street has sidewalks but no streetlights (Orange County), the other side has streetlights but no sidewalks (Los Angeles County). Your mother trains you to always say you live in Whittier, on account of it is the hometown of President Nixon, whom your mother worked to help elect. It also has a college, from which President Nixon graduated. La Habra has a lot of Mexicans. Not that we're better than Them, says your mother, but we're Whittier people.

In Whittier, you have a real dining-room table. Your mother calls it a dining-room suite. The suite is made of some heavy wood, ashy brown with little black flecks. The table comes with a couple of leaves, stretching it to seat about eight hundred. The style is Mediterranean, with six matching chairs and a sideboard that, your mother says, nearly gave the furniture delivery man a hernia. She is proud of this fact, her expensive dining-room suite bringing a man to his knees, literally. Now, she says, she can Entertain.

Entertaining means Parties. Your mother likes the minor holidays, Saint Patrick's Day, Memorial Day. One Halloween, the dining-room table is covered with a black paper tablecloth, orange crepe paper streamers twist away from the chandelier, not crystal, but cut glass, bought on time from a furniture store next to the Polar Palace, where you sometimes go ice skating, hoping someone will ask you to skate. Your mother has spent the last two days making Sweet and Sour Meatballs, liver pâté, and a lot of other grown-up food. The night of the party she is dressed in red leotards, black felt tail, and horns.

You ask your mother, Are you a devil, or what?

Your mother says, *The* Devil, sweetheart.

The Whittier dining room is still the kitchen side of the living room, but the living room is bigger than in the Sherman Oaks apartment. It is Fancy. It has burnt orange shag carpeting. On the windows facing the patio are gold brocade curtains that are tied back with thick gold cords with tassels. You like to tickle the dog's nose with the tassel, making him sneeze.

You are not allowed to leave anything on the table. You do your homework on the Formica breakfast bar in the kitchen, where your handwriting improves, and where you eat breakfast and dinner six days a week and on all non-Holidays and all non–Other Special Occasions.

The Other Special Occasions included Sunday dinner, birthday dinners, graduation dinners, and the few times you have a boy over to dinner. You can count the number of times you have a boy over to dinner on one hand. You can count the number of boys you actually like who come to dinner on one finger.

Jeff is the summer of eighth grade going into ninth. He is perfect because he is one of three boys in the ninth grade who is taller than you. Together, you make Tie-dye T-shirts and make out in the pool when your mother is out at the A&P. Jeff introduces you to hickeys and shoplifting. He knows the meaning of all the lyrics on the soundtrack of *Hair*.

Jeff has hair to his shoulders, streaked with auburn from the sun. Your mother says she doesn't like it, it makes him a hippy pot-smoking flower child, but once you saw her hold it back for him while he was leaning to get a drink of water from the tap at the sink. When you do this you are told to get a glass.

Another time your mother chases Jeff around the kitchen, trying to put his hair in pigtails, while you take pictures with your Instamatic. After you get the pictures back your mother says you shouldn't have taken pictures. You humiliated him.

When Jeff eats over, it is always in the dining room. Having what your mother calls a beau is a Special Occasion. You are never sure if Jeff is your beau or just your friend, and neither is Jeff. You worry, because according to your mother, he has to be one or the other. If he kisses you, he is a beau. But what if he also talks about other girls he has kissed? Other *boys* he has kissed? You ask your mother. She says, Just don't let him touch you above your knees or below your shoulders. That's for after you're married. You ask her this while she is sewing you a halter dress, backless, pink gingham. Sexy, you think, but you're not quite sure.

Dinner in the dining room always has beef in it. It is always white, green, and brown—potatoes, vegetables, and the beef. Or it's something that takes forever to cook. Beef Stroganoff, something that needs to simmer. There are Pop 'n' Fresh rolls in a basket, coddled in a cloth napkin that matches the Linen. The Linen is now bought at a department store.

The last time Jeff has dinner at your house he has already found a new girl that he likes, a girl one grade older who, it is rumored, Puts Out. You don't Put Out, you've obeyed your mother. Of all the things you must do to make a boy like you, Putting Out, the one thing he would like you to do above all others, is exactly the thing you must never do. Your mother says it's a little like holding a dog treat just above the dog's nose, so he can smell it but never quite reach it. You say, Yeah, but am I the treat or the person holding the treat? Both, says your mother.

No matter where your family eats, your father never knows what to say. He is an engineer. He can rebuild a sports car from the lug nuts up, but has trouble with simple conversation. No problem, usually, because your mother does all the talking. All the planning, all the shopping, all the cooking, all the table setting, all the serving. On the last night Jeff has dinner at your house, the last night he kisses you, although you will hold a torch for him well into college, where he becomes an art major and the lover of a man ten years his senior, your father attempts a joke.

"What's a wild goose?"

"I don't know, Dad, what's a wild goose?"

"About this much off center." He holds up his thumb and forefinger, displaying an invisible inch.

Jeff goes har-har-har. Phony? You can't tell. You don't get it. Jeff is sitting across from you. You catch his eye, mouth the words "I don't get it." He rolls his eyes. He mouths something back, he spells something, three letters, *a-s-s,* partly cupping his hand. You struggle to understand.

You ask your mother, What does an ass have to do with a goose?

Jeff rounds his shoulders, collapsing in on himself like a Halloween pumpkin past its prime. Your mother has a laugh like a machine gun. Your father blushes, mute.

At your birthday dinner, a few months later, there is a present at your place, beside your crystal water glass: *How to Get a Teenage Boy and What to Do with Him When You Get Him.* Not let your father tell jokes, you think, although that seems to be the least of your problems.

When your mother gets the itch to remodel, she has the living room extended to make a real dining room. There are now two steps up and a sliding glass door leading out to the patio. The construction guys arrive a little after seven in the morning and sometimes stay until dinner. Sometimes, you come home from swim team in the afternoon to find the main construction guy having a beer with your mother.

In 1971 there is a huge earthquake, one that will make world news. Most earthquakes are like train rides, but this one feels as if you're standing on a carpet that's being shaken out by unseen hands. You and your mother lunge for the door between the kitchen and the dining room at the same time. You stand there, you two, wedged shoulder to shoulder in the door frame, looking out the sliding glass door, watching while the surface of the swimming pool gathers itself into a tidal wave. You watch while the water slops over the side of the pool, runs down the patio, and sloshes against the sliding glass door, where it seeps beneath the door, drenching the burnt orange shag. Your mother, not a native Californian, worries to the point of insomnia about mildew for weeks. Once, getting up in the middle of the night to use the bathroom, you catch her in her olive green quilted bathrobe, down on her hands and knees, sniffing at the carpet.

Senior year, you and most of your friends are not invited to the prom. The Cool Crowd, the soshes, has decided that the prom is only for losers, and as you are in the Second Coolest Crowd, you decide the same thing. You are relieved, since, as your mother says, There is no one Decent on the horizon anyway.

The one boy who she has decided is Decent is Steve, the

older brother of one of your friends. Steve has already graduated and gone away to college in Colorado. Your mother buys you special stationery so you can write him letters at his dorm. Steve has had the same girlfriend for years, but she has a terminal disease, so there is hope for you. Steve actually answers your letters. He addresses you Hey Foxy! Your mother puts you on Dr. Stillman's diet, hard-boiled eggs and dietetic Jell-O, for when Steve comes home for the summer.

In the meantime, your mother decides you should host a dinner party the night of the prom. She will let each of your guests have a glass of Chablis if you help her plan the menu. You know what this means: cooking. Your mother has forbidden you to take typing in school because, she says, you are destined for Greater things. You secretly feel the same way about cooking.

You and your mother have a fight. You are not going to help plan the menu. You want to know why you can't just eat *food,* why does it always have to be a menu. You don't give a shit about one measly glass of Chablis. You use that word, *shit.* She slaps you across the face. You surprise yourself by slapping her right back. Your fingers leave stripes on her cheek. You say you don't want a dinner party. You say if she's so hot to have a dinner party, she should have one for her own friends and leave yours alone. She says you're an ingrate. You wail, Stop prosecuting me! Your mother's anger dissolves, diluted by amusement.

It's *persecuting,* she says. You're not as smart as you think you are, she says, and I thank the dear Lord for that.

You don't help with the menu, but get your glass of wine anyway. The afternoon of the prom is warm, the evening rose-colored. Even in this stupid suburb (you already know that Whittier, La Habra, whatever you want to call it is a place made for leaving) the evening smells of orange blossoms and possibilities, the kind of evening that, for the rest of your life, for reasons you will never understand, makes you ache. What you will understand is that this kind of evening also made your mother ache, and that's why she cooked.

You have seven friends over. You wear your pink gingham halter dress. Your mother has made lasagna, which she calls la-zag-na, thinking she's funny, a tossed green salad, garlic bread, and Dutch Chocolate Whip 'n' Chill for dessert. You eat off her bone china, use her silver service, then pile into her car, a 1964 Ford Galaxy convertible. You drink sloe gin and 7-Up, you cruise Whittier Boulevard, then cruise the high school, you get so drunk you throw up over the side of your mother's car. You take the car through the all-night, do-it-yourself car wash, spraying chunks of ricotta cheese off the side of the car. You vow to get out of Whittier, La Habra, whatever you want to call it, and never come back.

You go to college, a private college in Los Angeles, thirty minutes away in light traffic. At college, there are many Decent boys on the horizon. More Our Ilk, says your mother.

Your mother keeps track of your boyfriends by their fathers' professions. Mr. Golden West Broadcasting has a father who's the head of production there. Mr. Sunkist's father is vice president. There is also a Mr. Neurosurgeon.

When you talk to your mother on the phone she says, I can't keep your boyfriends straight! She always wants you to bring them home for dinner. You don't, because you can't. Mainly because Mr. Golden West Broadcasting, Mr. Sunkist, and Mr. Neurosurgeon are not your boyfriends. They are boys you know from a class or they are the boyfriends of your new sorority sisters. You pretend they are yours, because you know hearing about them will make your mother happy, and she is.

You should have known something was up when no one was invited to Thanksgiving. Thanksgiving is your mother's favorite holiday. It required days of menu-planning and shopping, getting up in pre-dawn darkness to put in the turkey. It required inviting Family, who drank more than they ate, and were sent stumbling to their cars with paper plates bowed with leftovers.

But this year, it is just you and your father and your mother. Your mother isn't feeling well. She has one of her headaches. She sits at her usual place at the head of the table, trying to slide a mound of stuffing onto her fork, then working to bring the fork to her mouth. She makes it look as difficult as a party trick. If you were either a child or an adult, you would notice that she is not right. But you are seventeen, and only have eyes for yourself.

Twenty minutes after you arrive at your dorm your father calls to tell you what he couldn't bring himself to tell you at the dining-room table: in a week, your mother will have exploratory brain surgery.

You ask your father, Will she be okay?

Your father says, Of course.

After the surgery, the surgeon comes out in his greens. He looks at you, but he talks to your father. The surgeon says, "How old is she?"

Your mother doesn't die right away, but her personality does. The tumor was shaped like a plate of spaghetti minus the plate.

To remove as much of it as possible, they needed to take a goodly amount of healthy brain tissue. *Goodly* is the surgeon's word. You ask your father, in the car on the way home, What does he mean by goodly? A sound comes out of your father, like someone gasping for air.

Your mother comes home from the hospital. She stops cooking, but she refuses to stop smoking. You do not have Friday classes, so you come home every weekend on Thursday afternoon. You come home every Thursday afternoon to find her sitting in the kitchen, at the Formica breakfast bar, trying to get the cigarette to stay between her fingers. She wraps a rubber band around the top of her index and middle fingers to keep them closed.

You drive her to chemo on Friday. Afterward, you stop for a box of glazed doughnuts, her lunch. She sits at the dining-room table while you tell her about your boyfriends. It doesn't matter that this is not an Occasion. The way you make it sound, a marriage proposal is just around the corner.

You do have a date with a boy from your oceanography class. He is Mr. Head Lettuce; his father owns a corporate farm in Bakersfield. You don't tell your mother about Mr. Head Lettuce. You don't know why. You have the feeling she won't understand that his father isn't a hick with manure beneath his fingernails; also, you make Mr. Head Lettuce cry, telling him how your mother is dying, only she doesn't really know it. She knows it, then she forgets it.

You and Mr. Head Lettuce stand in line for six hours to see *The Exorcist.* It gives you a lot of time to talk.

You tell him how, just last week, your mother told you she

wanted Fun Mom put on her headstone. You were sitting at the dining-room table. She was eating her glazed doughnuts straight from the box, flecks of glaze on her chin.

Your mother says, Aren't I the Funnest Mom you know?

You say, You are.

Your mother says, Don't humor me because I look like a plucked chicken. Do I look like a plucked chicken?

In the first days after her surgery, your mother gamely bought a wardrobe of turbans, all in shades of orange—apricot, squash, and tangerine. Now, she doesn't bother. Her hair is gone. On one side of her head is the scar, scabby, a rusty croquet wicket. Scratching it has become a bad habit, something she does when she isn't smoking or eating.

Mr. Head Lettuce whispers, Are you close to her, your mother, I mean?

You say, I don't know. Sure.

You mean, Yes. You mean, No. You mean, N/A. It's like asking if your left leg is close to your right leg.

You never go out with Mr. Head Lettuce again. No one is touching you above your knees or below your shoulders. Your mother should be relieved, but you know this is not what she had in mind. No one is touching you at all.

Then, a miracle happens.

Suddenly, there is a Boy, Mr. Orthodontist from Palos Verdes. His name is also Jeff. You meet him at a fraternity mixer and you hear through the grapevine that he is going to ask you out, and—this is the miracle—the grapevine was right, he does ask you out. He asks you out for the night of your eighteenth birthday.

You are expected home for your birthday, which falls on a Saturday that year. You come home in the afternoon to find the dining-room table already set. The gold brocade curtains are open, sun filters through the dark pink bougainvillea that covers the trellis over the patio. The table is covered with a gold table-cloth, the cut crystal is out, two glasses at each place, one for water, one for wine.

At your place, oddly, there is a stack of identical envelopes. Birthday cards that came in the mail? You don't think you know that many people.

Your mother shuffles in with another card for the pile. She is supposed to be getting better, your mother, but something in you knows that you don't get better from this; the most you can hope for is not getting worse.

You flip through the cards, recognizing her palsied hand-writing on each envelope. You and your mother understand what has happened at the same moment. Apparently, she couldn't remember whether she'd gotten you a card or not.

Your mother says, They are all from me.

Dinner is prime rib with baked potato. Sour cream and chives, only your mother brings out Cool Whip and chives. You look at your father over the table. He will not meet your gaze. He slices open his potato, then leaves it empty. Your mother by-passes her potato, spooning Cool Whip directly into her mouth.

You, like your mother, are a woman with itches. Suddenly, you itch to get away. Away from this dining-room table, away from this tract house, this suburb, this life. You stand up, in the middle of your birthday dinner and say, I have a date. I have to go.

Your father says, Your mother worked for a week on this meal.

Your mother says, Let her go.

It is the last thing your mother ever says to you.

You date Mr. Orthodontist twice, then set him up with a sorority sister he eventually marries. Six days after your birthday, your father calls, crying incoherently—you think it's an obscene phone call—to say that your mother has gone into a coma. She lives like that for a day and a night. A month after your mother's death, your father sells her dining-room suite. You note he sells it at a loss.

# MONA SIMPSON

The house had a polished dining table in the living room, flanked by sconces, but it was a sham. I remember it opened out only twice, after funerals. It was much the same as the front door with its attendant coat closet and the Polynesian room in the basement, where joy-colored lights tinted dusty exotic cocktail glasses over the Kon-Tiki bar, and a mounted sailfish camouflaged the door to the root cellar. Improbably, a slot machine reigned in the corner, stalled on a flush of pears.

These were relics, from an earlier, more boisterous time in the house's life, when guests parked on the long semicircular front drive, clacked and shushed in the front door, through the kitchen, down the stairs to dance in the Polynesian room, to the Merry Macs, Lawrence Welk, Benny Goodman, Guy Lombardo and His Royal Canadians. I have forgotten to mention that there was a Victrola and a ledge of thick LPs.

That era was long over. By the time I lived there, it was a grandmother's house, with the unexpected jangly addition of children. We were left there for spells while our parents tried to untangle their forbiddingly adult lives. There were three of us. Sometimes just one of us would be there, sometimes two, sometimes all. Sometimes siblings, sometimes cousins. In my grandmother's presence we each became different in the house. We shared her bafflement toward our parents as we watched them drive away in their cars. It seemed our grandparents had never been so dangerously young. We didn't know yet if we would be.

We lived—most of our time—in the kitchen, around or beneath the table, which was aluminum and Formica in the style of the day, gray-flecked with tubular silver legs that felt good to tangle your feet around.

In the morning, we woke to the minute sounds of my grandmother shuffling and dividing, dealing out her cards on that table.

Breakfast was what we wanted. Sometimes we wanted just pie from last night, my grandmother's one-crust fruit pies with their dark lace tops. Once in a while, there would be pancakes, currants warm and running inside, from the small bush outside. When it was raining, she would have something called oefflaven already in the oven, in a cast-iron pan. More like a popover than a pancake, it rose with peaks of air, and she served it with powdered sugar and cinnamon. For years, afterward, we tried to find the recipe, but she had never written it down. Sometimes we didn't know what we wanted and then we got eggs, beautifully cooked, the ruffled waves centered on the green plate, with four even quarters of toast at the sides. To get eggs that taste like that now people who care enough go to outdoor markets at dawn or drive to small free-range poultry farms to buy fertile odd-colored eggs, with names like Araucana or Japanese Silkies. None of us do. Of course, everyone eats fewer eggs now anyway. Probably a whole generation of women were accomplished short-order cooks as my grandmother was, without ever considering it a skill.

The kitchen was a big, perfectly square room, the easiest configuration for symmetry and consoling order. The wreath of fluorescent light centered the ceiling exactly and stuttered on when you flicked the switches by either door.

The vast, white stove faced the deep kitchen sink and its window, which telescoped a deep yard and beyond that fields, which changed crops in the course of our lives there. First cow corn, then alfalfa, then hay. For a while after, nothing. Now, pavement.

The refrigerator faced the mangle, an obsolete, beautiful, white enamel four-legged trouser press, on which my grandmother kept her thriving African violets.

The two west corners were doors: one to a little hall that gave onto the staircase, the living room, and more halls, to the den and downstairs bedroom; the other to the back entry, where the dog slept and my grandmother hung his long leashes and collar, and all our outdoor clothes.

The southeast corner held the evil closet with the broom and the wastepaper basket. We didn't have garbage exactly. Wastepaper was collected in a brown grocery bag with a neat cuff folded down from the top and burned outside every Friday night in a can. Food scraps were composted for the garden, and most everything else was collected in the garage until the day we drove out to the dump.

In the northeast corner, there was the telephone, a party line and the only one in the house, which rested on the counter. A chair resided between that counter and the refrigerator and somehow in that small recessed square, one felt a kind of privacy even as my grandmother moved over the stove and boys stood gulping milk, in one long drink. There was a drawer beneath the phone, with paper and three-inch sharpened pencils, old calendars, rubber bands, erasers, ancient grocery lists.

We fiddled with these things, talking to our parents on the phone, whispering, *When?* Yes. Steak. Blueberry. No. Everything here was fine. It was just that we wanted to go home.

I pictured where they were—the other side of time, a flatter light, bright things new. I was missing time even then.

The first few minutes after our parents, when we watched the car until it was gone or when they hung up, we took time to adjust. It was the country here. We heard the sounds of outside and no other people. And the sounds of machines. Electricity jolting the refrigerator and the electric clock. There was also a German carved cuckoo clock that chimed every quarter hour. The small radio. The regular ticking chirp of the baby goose in the corner. Soft, repetitive sounds, varieties of ticking. The gosling's peeping, not plaintive but soothing even to itself like the sound of knitting. My grandmother's shuffling and dealing.

Animals were always a part of our life there and they, too, lived in the kitchen. Our young parents bought us dogs and bunnies and baby ducks (one of which turned out to be a goose) on Easter, and when they were too much for us to take care of, they landed at my grandmother's house the same way we did. The bunny and the goose lived in the kitchen until they were big enough to go outside. The rabbit slept in my grandmother's old sock. The gosling had its own cardboard box, with holes just big enough for its beak. The goose grew huge soon.

Time went slow here between breakfast and lunch. For hours I'd draw under the kitchen table, when I was little, or tangle under the tent the white sheet made when my grandmother ironed, on the board that came out from the wall. Her nylons carried a dry burnt smell.

The boys and the animals always wanted to go outside and so I did too, at first to follow, then just for itself. My grandmother let us out when we wanted, as she did the dog. She remained in the kitchen while we ran. We would see her through the windows, doing the few chores left. Even in a house with children, my grandmother seemed to find herself with too much time between chores. She called us in for lunch.

Often at lunchtime, hoboes would come to the door from the 11:55, having made their way up the hill from the railroad. The train was regular. Somehow even the hoboes knew to use the back door. My grandmother didn't invite them in to sit down with us, but she'd fix them a plate of food to eat on the porch. Maybe a liverwurst sandwich divided into four on a square green plastic plate, which had once been a giveaway at the gas station. Plastic gives a taste to food. Her mother's German china, white plates as thin as watery paper, were stacked on her top cupboard boards so they looked like a tiered wedding cake, but she never used them. Not for us. When the hoboes left, she packed them another lunch in a paper bag, and included dented cans her cousin got free from the railroad company.

She baked in the afternoon in that kitchen, scattering flour

right on the table. She collected hickory nuts and picked out
their small soft meat, putting her glasses on to see right.

Dinner was a strange mix of work and convenience. It is hard
to describe. There were always things fresh from the garden in
summer, things pickled, mixed in with the bright variety of food
from cans, packages, or frozen boxes. Many little bowls set out.
What we liked. My cousin loved oranges, and when he was
there, she sliced a bowlful for the table.

The old white sink was huge and where we had our baths, one
at a time. They took place after dinner, and most of the year there
was still light out. I remember the bitter shampoo rinsings under
that spout. You sat with your knees up and could see all the way to
the copse of pine in the back, past lilacs, past my grandmother's
garden, with its birdbath, its bleeding hearts, its lady's slippers.

We were washed one at a time, so you watched the others,
how strange they looked, older and dumb with wet-down hair.

Before bed at night, the last thing, we sat barefoot at that
table, eating a bowl of Special K, conscious of the clock.

Eventually, our parents all came back to claim us. Usually
they ran in late in the day. They sat down, young again too—we
forgot every time, this was their house first, before ours, it was
the place they had been children. They ate their mother's warm
pie, letting its intricacy unwind in the mouth, drinking milk the
same as we had, but only now. They needed the other, what they
found out far away, first.

That clean aluminum and Formica oval was the scene of more
important events than either the department store dining table

in the living room or the French cherry wood round table from our great-grandmother, in the basement, on which my grandmother kept her tools.

We ate dinners there, regular summer daylight supper and Christmas dinner before midnight Mass.

My grandmother learned of her grandchildren there: one's dropout, an arrest, another's death.

I remember spying in the kitchen, opening the drawers—a changed room in a new light—when my grandmother was in the hospital.

She died in 1979. The house was worth, I believe, $35,000.

For a while our parents kept it, then it was sold. A young couple lived there, and they were said to paint the walls funny colors. Once, visiting from graduate school in the winter snow, I peeked inside through those kitchen windows on a Tuesday night and slipped off the drainpipe, wetting my East Coast big city shoes. The walls were painted red. A plaid couch. Except for appliances, the kitchen didn't seem to be a kitchen anymore.

Then, a few years later, the land was sold to a developer for a Wal-Mart. But before they could build they had to get rid of the house and especially the yard's tall, almost century-old trees.

The fire department used the house for its drills. They'd light it on fire, put it out, and start all over again. Neighbors across the street whom we'd known all our lives scavenged everything useful or valuable: the stove, the refrigerator, and the washer. My grandmother had never owned a dryer. She hung clothes out on a line of string between two hickory trees.

The woman across the road took out all the old crystal doorknobs with a screwdriver, carrying the haul in a hammock of her apron. My aunt would have liked to ask for one but felt afraid to. "Don't think she'd give it to me," she said.

Eventually the trees were burnt down, the house was empty, gone. Blacktop was laid.

My cousin takes his new friends from the church. "See here, this spot in the parking lot, there was a fifty-foot-high oak, and in the store all the way in the back, where the sewing shit is, that's where I slept. Yah. That was my room.

"Where the pets are, goldfish and crap, right about there, birds, that was Gram's kitchen. She was always in her kitchen."

Half the old neighbors are still there. Only the east side of the road was burned, razed, and rebuilt; the other houses are pretty much as they were in the forties and fifties, with many of the same people in them. They are waiting, I've been told, for the commercial development to obliterate them, too. They know enough to hold on to their land.

I've been back to my hometown several times since but I still haven't been out to see.

# SALLIE TISDALE

*G*randma Stelle is a very small woman, with lavender hair curled around her little wrinkled face like sunset clouds. She smells of face powder and cigarettes, and waves the smoke away from her with a lac-quered cigarette holder. I have to sit next to Grandma at the annual fam-ily birthday dinner, the one with all my gray-haired aunts and uncles. I don't know why she wants me there; she usually ignores me, but this time she suggests it.

The birthday dinner is held in the banquet room of a country steak house around a long rectangular table. The room is cold and echoes a lit-tle under the high beams of the ceiling. The walls are rough wood, deco-rated with horseshoes, checkered curtains, and mountain scenes in elaborate brass-colored frames. Sputtering white candles in nubbly red glasses sit on the plastic red-white checked tablecloth. The waitress, smelling of sweat, brushes against me with her ruffled apron and calls me

*hon. I play at making rivers of gravy on my mashed potatoes and kick-*
*ing my brother under the table, caught up in the fragments of noise around*
*me. We are eating fried chicken, and Grandma loves fried chicken.*

*She picks up a drumstick in her fingers, manicured red nails ex-*
*tended out away from the sticky juice, and nibbles delicately through the*
*crispy skin. Bite by bite she eats the dark meat, dribbling a little oily pud-*
*dle onto her plate. With steady, tiny nips and pecks, her dentures clicking*
*quietly, she turns the drumstick like a cob of corn until it's clean. She*
*looks away from me, brings her napkin up to dab at her red lips, smiles*
*at someone I can't see, and in one hidden motion slips the bone onto my*
*plate. And reaches for another piece.*

We are going to Grandma's house, as we often do, Mom, Dad,
my brother, my sister, and me. It's a long drive, but I don't mind
the car. I'm used to beauty on this drive, a splendid, moving
beauty. First the volcanic plain, undulant with empty hills. By
daylight they run for miles, without a single sharp edge in them.
In moonlight their bare skins look like the hides of rhinoceroses,
rough and warm. Lonely rock walls climb the hills and disappear
without reason, and here and there I see a scatter of white beehives and the polka-dots of sheep. Then lush carpets of pine and
fir, full and dark, with spiky teeth of enormous granite towers
rising out of the trees, like dragon lands in unmapped places. In
the middle is the mountain, immense and solitary, covered in
snow, visible from every turn. I know stories about this mountain, how some people think superior beings live inside—tall,
slender people in white robes who play extravagant, alien bells.
Sometimes I see strange clouds around the peak.

We drive to Grandma's house, through the plain, past the forests, up into the steep hills near the mountain, rolling down the highway in our tired station wagon, past the sheep, the beehives, the mountain, past the dark ribbon of the river, shallow, fast, and cold, and past the railroad and the trains.

Grandma's house is perched halfway up a long, steep hill; the whole bright town steps block by block up a slope, facing the mountain. The houses are built on levels, first floors turning into attics, front porches hanging off in space, bedrooms opening into yards—a crooked cartoon town with fountains on every corner, making a ceaseless murmur, bubbling out water that looks like silver and tastes the way silver should taste. Mountain water, come all the way down and up again. Sometimes there is grass and roses, and sometimes there is snow, great heaps of snow shoved up against the houses, above the windowsills, packing them in. Always there is light.

Dad pulls off the highway into town and drives along the wide street until he comes to a small church made of darkened wood planks and embroidered with wisteria vines. At the church, he turns up, straight up, and I spin around in my seat to stare out the back window at what we are leaving behind, the receding church below, the lines of railroad tracks beside the winding river, the toothbrush silhouettes of trees beside the cockeyed houses, until we reach the top and turn the corner on Grandma's street, and park.

Before we arrive Grandma lays down plastic runners on the carpet, marking the children's required path, and covers the huge sofa and armchairs with crinkly plastic sheets. We march in single file like soldiers, through the living room, down a short hall, and into the shiny kitchen, where suddenly we are two stories high. Out the kitchen door are two flights of wooden stairs down to the sloping flower garden. Flying straight out from the tiny porch like a flying buttress over the sea is a long double clothesline on a pulley. The spotless, pale kitchen is split by sun, the light unencumbered by trees; below Grandma's house is the slope of the town—the backyard neighbor's house, and his neighbor below that, falling off into the sky, the forest, the plain, and far away, looking on, the white mountain. Whenever I think I've left it behind it is there again, closer than before, a cold luxury of light.

"Go on down to the basement, now," someone says, and we go, and stay.

The long flight of wooden basement stairs descends to the center of a clean cement floor. The main room is lit by a bare bulb with a silver pull chain that shakes the bulb, making the shadows flicker for a long time after someone turns it on. In dimness we come slowly down the stairs, gooseflesh on our arms, into the spotlight. The movement of the bulb illuminates our faces in new, strange ways; our faces become anyone's faces, all faces, no longer familiar. We step off the last of the wooden stairs and someone in the kitchen notices we've left the basement door open and closes it, and the square of sun disappears.

From visit to visit, day to day, nothing changes. We explore, wearing T-shirts and sneakers, shorts in the summer and jeans in the winter, never warm enough. The walls are hidden by piles of boxes, cupboards, dressers, bureaus and trunks, a wicker pram, a big highboy decorated with faded paintings of geese and ducks, a dusty steel safe, and heavy things lost in shadow, submerging me. Grandma saves everything; she keeps it here, keeps the house, keeps it all.

I am more than two years younger than Bruce. Bruce and I are sturdy, competent children, and look so much alike, with our brown hair and green eyes, that we sometimes pass for twins. Bruce is scared of ants, and girls, in that order, something he only tells me. But he's brave, too; I admire his bravery; he takes my father's blows without tears. I know how much he hates Pop Warner football, too, but he never mentions quitting; we both know that's not an option. Susan, barely a year younger than me, isn't brave at all. She's squeamish, chubby, pale and black-haired—she's the one left out, the baby. At home, Bruce and I often tease Susan, with bugs and gory stories, or simply ditch her when we've had enough. In the basement at Grandma's house the three of us form a band. We wander through the dim, cold rooms, round and round. "Don't touch anything," Grandma calls down from the kitchen, a little alarmed at our distant sounds, and we promise we won't, and she closes the door again.

We try again and again to open the safe, flipping the dial through endless combinations, and pry unsuccessfully at the locks on the trunks. We trace the painted ducks with our fingers. Bruce, being brave, looks in the darkest corners and under the stairs, where we long ago hid the only toy we have here, a battered red scooter that belonged to my father when he was a boy. At the end of the stairs are two small rooms with a tiny bathroom between them, smelling of rust. Grandma calls them the guest rooms. Each has a musty twin bed with a chenille bedspread that feels damp under my hands. There are bookshelves in the guest rooms, old paperbacks and hardback novels with cover paintings of masted sailing ships blown by storm and scarred gunmen atop rearing horses. On top of the largest bookshelf sits a pair of tiny bronze shoes with stiff, metallic laces tied in bows.

I go upstairs to ask my mother about them, and find her in the kitchen making coffee. She says they are my father's baby shoes. Upstairs, the mantelpieces are covered with porcelain animals and rococo clocks, vases and picture frames, paperweights and china dolls. I follow my mother through the living room into the front bedroom, where Grandma is searching for something in her strange trousseau. The bedrooms are full of hampers, big jewelry boxes, cupboards, valises and hatboxes, piles of blankets, mountains of ironed and folded linen, closets stuffed with clothing, and a chiffonier, each drawer filled with nightgowns and bathrobes. In the den is a rolltop desk covered with files, a wardrobe filled with several sets of china packed in quilted covers, shelves packed with dark, bound books. In the main bedroom and both bathrooms the long vanity tables are covered with lace runners and doilies, big pink boxes of powder, vials of cologne, hand lotion, hair spray, and creams. Nothing is ever threadbare or worn, and nothing is ever new. Nothing changes.

Grandma's small bent body barely clears the pile of blankets beside the bed. She has red lips and yellow teeth, and her hands are swollen and thick; her fingers look like chicken bones, clutching a cigarette.

She turns and sees me standing there in the doorway, watching, and sighs, white smoke dribbling out of her nose. Her intense dark eyes are like the shiny glass eyes of teddy bears, which I hate. My stuffed animals have soft cloth eyes and long lashes. She stares at me a moment and says, "Go on down to the basement, now." My mother doesn't say a word, only looks at me, and I go.

Downstairs, I sit on the bedspread a long time, holding the weight of the tiny shoes in my hands. How could a baby wear such heavy shoes? I wonder. They've made my father a weary man. He has trouble waking up in the morning, and often my mother has to coax him out of bed, and he sleeps in his chair in the late afternoon before dinner, and he sleeps again after dinner, laid out flat on the sofa like a corpse while we sit on the rug in front of him, watching television.

We are all quiet at once. The airless clutter slowly fills with sound—the lack of sound, the sound of someone making no noise, someone holding very still, subterranean, buried. I jump up, and grab the scooter.

Round and round and round we ride, counting the laps, the short oval laps, counting one, two.

"That's four!"

*round and round*

Upstairs, the grown-ups are in the den. My grandmother is at the center, prim, elegant, smoking with a restrained grace. My grandfather leans back in his dark brown leather armchair, holding a glass of whiskey on ice. My father sits in the smaller armchair. He is my grandmother's only child, her destiny, her hope. He lives in a house his father built, next door to the house where he was raised. His hand shakes a little as he reaches for his drink. My mother sits nearby—nervous, homely, laughing at every little joke.

She is fond of a photograph from her college days—a dozen anonymous young people on the grass, one blond and one brunette cheerleader leaning on the football captain's arm in the center of the picture, and my mother alone in her patch of grass, grinning, pleased to be so close. I know, because she told me when I asked, that she proposed to my father herself, tired of waiting, and when he refused she left him, but then there was the war, two years of worry and a few cryptic letters, and when he came back he was different, he was ready. In the wedding picture she looks happy, really happy, standing upright and proud in a fashionable dress, and he looks thin and dark and serious. A year later Bruce was born, and in a photo taken shortly afterward, Dad holds my newborn brother in the crook of one big hand, and a can of beer in the other. He is already getting fat.

Upstairs they're playing cards, they're drinking highballs and smoking cigarettes, one after the other, so that the small den fills with a high thin blue haze, and under the sound of murmuring laughter is the clatter of ice and the mumble of the television.

"That's eight!"

*round and round*

And the scooter flies out from under my sister. My brother and I are sitting on the bottom step keeping score. The scooter goes one way and my little sister the other on the hard, cold, cement floor. She scrapes her knee and it starts to bleed and of course she cries, she always cries; she's weak but we don't torment her. Here we help.

Later, when my son is born, he is the first grandchild, the first great-grandchild. When he is a week old, my parents drive hundreds of miles to bring Grandma to visit. Grandma sits propped by pillows in an armchair and I hand my infant to her so Dad can take pictures. After a few minutes, he begins to wake and whimper—the mewling puppy sound of hungry babies—and I reach for him. But Grandma pulls back, guarding him, staring. She says, "Boys don't cry," and again, singsong, "Boys don't cry," staring me down.

It doesn't occur to me to go up the steps and ask for a Band-Aid. My mother would be glad to help, I know, but I also know my mother has her hands full here and I prefer to let her be. I improvise with toilet paper and a piece of cloth we find somewhere, until my sister quiets down.

Lunch is melted cheese sandwiches on white bread, served on paper plates at the kitchen table. Afterward, I ask my mother if I can take a magazine with me to read. She gives me *The Saturday Evening Post,* and I sit on the bottom basement step a while and meditate on the pictures of astronauts and royalty.

At home, my brother and I go to the movies every Saturday, walking alone down the street to the theater for the matinee. In every scary movie there is a basement scene, a moment when some doomed fool creeps cautiously down those stairs. I don't like scary movies, but it's not because of Grandma's basement. Even in the long-forgotten fruit cellar, hidden behind a heavy door, I'm not afraid; I've quit feeling afraid and feel other things instead. The thick plank shelves are cobwebbed and musty, covered with cloudy Mason jars. When I pick one up, odd shapes move heavily in the thick syrup, like captured elves. These are the basement's bones, the hidden things, put away. They are so dead they can't even be ghosts.

I sit in the hushed cold of Grandma's basement and read my magazine and make up stories, and disappear.

I vaguely knew from things I'd heard my parents say that the tall, bald man I called my grandfather wasn't really that at all, that my real grandfather had been dead a long time. Grandma married and was widowed, and then remarried and was widowed again, and remarried once more, all before I was born. When this third husband died, Grandma sold their house and moved in next door to my parents, back into the house where my father was raised, where his real father killed himself. She brought all her things with her, a museum for the detritus of marriage. She filled the house next door, and she filled the walls and ceiling of the double garage in between, and she put some in the attic and some in my parents' little half basement, and some in the basement below her, a wretched coal bin hole, where the high soft bed from the basement bedroom moldered into a rat's nest of cotton dust.

A long time later, I have a daughter and take her to visit Grandma. She sits, as she sits every day, on the big sofa, smoking endlessly, a can of beer discreetly propped beside her, the barely chewed remains of the meal-on-wheels on the end table. She wears no makeup and her stained, faded housedress has cigarette burns in it. She leans forward to my daughter and says, "Give me a kiss now." My daughter presses back against my thighs, silent. Grandma leans a little closer. "If you give me a kiss I'll give you twenty dollars." I turn and leave, carrying my daughter on my hip, passing a tinted photograph of my brother at her age, smiling.

_At the end of the day, when it's time to go home, we children are called up from the basement at last, and we wearily climb the stairs and file like prisoners of war out to the car. Except me. I'm not going home this time; I'm checking out of here. I hide, and watch my father climb into the driver's seat and my mother lean in to shush my sister and pat my brother's arm. She doesn't notice that I'm gone, no one notices but Bruce. He presses his face against the window, mouth open. When he was very small, Grandma came to him, leaning forward with those knobby hands, and wrapped his face in plastic like the sofa, and he's spent all these years screaming for air, clawing at the mask. His screaming makes no sound. My mother climbs into the passenger seat and rolls down the window and Grandma and Grandpa stand on the stoop and wave good-bye— "Bye!"—and Mom waves good-bye—"Bye now!"—and Dad pulls away. He drives to the end of the block and turns the corner, and I know they're heading straight down the hills into the earth, down the long, long street that ends in a dark, silent church, round and round along the twisting roads to home._

_Out the kitchen door, to the porch, and sky. I climb up on the railing way above the garden, and loop my hands over the clothesline, and push away. Out I swing over the sunny green yard, swaying in the high blue sky, out above the steep hills._

_round and round_

_I dangle a moment, hearing the scurry of my grandmother's return, watching the mountain a few miles away, watching me. I hear a distant peal, deep and long. I'm a rocket, I'm a bird, I take wing. I'm snapping free, like my mother's clean white cotton sheets in the sweet cool breeze. My grandmother grabs the pulley and, squeak by squeak, tries to reel me in, but it's too late, I'm gone._

## COLIN HARRISON

We were in our twenties then and had been married a mere five months. We inspected the bedroom solemnly, trying to imagine ourselves sleeping and living in what was only a vacant room in a vacant house in Brooklyn, the floors dusty, the air stale. The building dated from 1883, but the old horsehair plaster was newly patched and painted around the Victorian mantel and walnut window moldings. My wife and I stood on the oak parquet, thinking of the unknowable lives lived in that room. Perhaps, in addition to babies and children and the cry of pleasure, there had also been malaise, suffering, death. It seemed only likely.

. . .

We populated the room slowly. Our first bed was a metal-framed piece of junk that I'd bought at an Iowa yard sale for ten dollars and spray-painted blue. Each post originally had a metal cap. One had been lost, and the previous owner had fashioned a poorly fitting replacement. Upon the final exertions of sex, the cap would vibrate against the post, ringing ridiculously. Our first child was conceived in that bed.

We put photographs on the mantel: wedding pictures, pictures of my wife's mother (dead at the age of forty-three from breast cancer), her grandmother (who had raised her, and still very much alive), her grandfather, her great-grandmother, my parents, and a picture of myself that I prized, in which I was running the mile relay in high school, about to hand off the baton—seventeen, all legs and lungs. On the floor we laid a silk rug we'd bought in India on our honeymoon. We'd had a Quaker wedding, in which the husband and wife sign a large, hand-inked certificate, which in turn is signed by all those present at the wedding. Ours, bordered by purple and green vines, contained about one hundred signatures on it, some slanting left, some right, some tightly inscribed or tiredly looped or brightly flourished, some scrawled by children, others shakily inscribed by octogenarians. We framed the certificate and put it on the wall, over my dresser, an English antique in which my wife's grandfather had stored his socks and underwear for almost fifty years.

· · ·

Our next bed was a French antique of sorts. My wife, six months pregnant, found it at a stoop sale in our Brooklyn neighborhood, arriving at home breathlessly with the news—"I found a bed, only two hundred dollars." The seller was a woman in her early fifties. Frosted hair, worldly as the Wife of Bath. The bed was lovely, but would it hold up? "Well," the woman said with a shrug, "my last husband weighed three hundred pounds, if that tells you anything."

It was while lying in this bed, late one February night, that my wife told me her water had broken. By now an empty bassinet sat expectantly at the foot of the bed, and a shelf had been given over to various baby-rearing books. My wife consulted one of these, then called her doctor. The next night I slept in that bed alone, exhausted, exultant, a new father. Three nights later my wife and baby daughter nursed happily and slept there. Three nights after that they were both back in the hospital, the baby yellow with jaundice, my wife still in pain from labor. Again I slept alone, fitfully. Three nights later baby and mother came home—healthy, we thought. Two nights later, we laid our baby on our bed and I knew, with an innate animal knowledge, that something was terribly wrong. We consulted another of the baby books on the shelf. I timed our daughter's fluttery respirations, which I calculated to be occurring more than ninety times a minute. *Seek medical attention immediately.* Back to the hospital went mother and daughter. Our ten-day-old daughter had pneumonia and was placed in an oxygen tent. My wife seemed inconsolable at first, then retreated to a far, deep place within herself, summoning a kind of hard-assed determination. The bedroom was now a vault of solitude, the bassinet empty again, the French bed a torturous place where I tossed, worried for my daughter, for my wife, for us.

. . .

Not so long after that, as our daughter made cooing noises from the crib, I stood in front of the framed wedding certificate and counted the people who had died. Several older relatives, some family friends. My own grandmother, who had starved herself to death in her nursing home, in despair over the death of her roommate of fifteen years. And now some of the married couples who had signed the certificate were divorced.

. . .

One July night my wife got pregnant again, in the French bed. Whereas the first time she had been nervous, this time she was proud and confident. In August her grandmother, who had raised her, died at the age of ninety-two. My wife went to the funeral home and spent some time alone with the body before it was cremated. Shortly after that she miscarried. It seemed that one death had caused another. Nana's ashes sat on the bedroom mantel—a plastic bag with chips of bone and an identifying medallion inside. My wife, intrepid in matters of the spirit, tasted some of the ashes of the woman who had fed and clothed and sheltered her. Later she cast the ashes in the waters of Long Island Sound from a sailboat.

We repaired to the French bed. What had been taken away could be seized back.

. . .

My wife had perhaps twenty pairs of shoes. I owned three pairs of shoes, and yet it was mine that she always tripped over on her way to the bathroom in the middle of the night. As the years went by, I got better about putting my shoes away.

. . .

When our son started to crawl, I found that I had a new habit. I picked stuff up in the house. Anything tiny. *Anything.* A friend told us that once, while baby-sitting a one-year-old, she had left the room for a moment and had come back to find the baby choking. She was terrified. She held the baby upside down but that didn't work. The choking continued, and in desperation she put her fingers into the baby's throat, finding a tiny piece of a leaf, as might be tracked onto a rug by a wet shoe. Instantly the baby was fine. Our friend was not, and years later I saw the fright on her face as she told me the story. So I picked things up. All of them went first into my pocket and then into the top drawer of my dresser in the bedroom, which was the best place I could think of. No child could get there. I picked things up for eighteen straight months and I never did this unconsciously. Pennies, tacks, apple seeds, dried corn kernels, bolts, screws, screw eyes, pen caps, pieces of felt torn from stuffed animals, buttons, marbles, pieces of yarn, orphaned caps to toothpaste and Chapstick, dried fragments of watercolor paints, nickels, the twisty thing from bread bags, feathers from the bedroom pillows, taxi receipts, wheels of toy cars, wheels of toy trains, pieces of orange peel, shards of seashell, bits of plastic, hairpins, straight pins, safety pins, dimes, paper clips, rubber bands, dried peas, Barbie shoes, Barbie combs, Barbie hair bands, Barbie brushes, needles, twigs, paint chips, beads of every color, fingernail clippings, broken pencil points—all went into the top drawer, right beneath the framed wedding certificate.

. . .

My wife and I continued to learn about each other in that bed, in that bedroom. In the dark, within the pressure of children and jobs and money, our appetites found new expression.

. . .

When we had dinner parties, the guests would deposit their coats in our bedroom. While downstairs, I could tell that they often lingered a moment or two upstairs, inspecting the room, glimpsing the many pictures on the mantel, staring at the bed, seeking the secret that is a marriage and a family. It gave me pleasure to know they were doing this.

. . .

The bedroom had a small color television, and among my most sublime relaxations was to watch professional football games on it while sitting on the bed, often drinking a Coke and eating a peanut-butter and honey and banana sandwich. Sometimes I even spread out the Sunday *New York Times* and read the sections between plays. Or I paid bills. It was on such an afternoon that my wife called frantically from the kitchen downstairs. I flew down the steps. Our son had fallen from the high kitchen step that leads to the backyard. He had hit his head badly and was now unconscious. I called the ambulance and we laid our son on the sofa. The ambulance arrived and left quickly with my son and wife. I needed to stay at home with our daughter. I drifted disconsolately upstairs to the bedroom and lay down on the bed, looking up at the ceiling cracks.

. . .

That spring, I noticed that the house had once had shutters on the back wall. All that was left were the hinge mounts and little pieces of iron embedded in the brick on either side of the windows—what was left of the shutter stays. From the bedroom window I tied a long piece of twine to each and dropped the twine down to the deck below. There I staked the strings into a planter. The back of the house looked like a strange acoustic instrument, with eight or ten lines running up the wall. We planted morning glories, which crawled vigorously upward, blooming in purple abundance. That summer, as a result of my regular watering, the vines reached the bedroom window, curling up and over the sill.

. . .

From time to time, I heard something downstairs in the middle of the night. A creak or a rattle or a noise. In these moments I would be aware that the intimacy and vulnerability of the bedroom—a place of sleep and sex and children's soft snoring—existed only as a result of brick walls, outdoor photoelectric lighting, window bars, and a double set of locked front doors. Lying in bed, my imagination moved like a phantom down the stairs, trying to match my memory of the sound with my knowledge of particular doors and windows and floorboards. What if someone was breaking in, *now*? I'd listen again, and if I thought I heard another noise, I'd force myself to get up in the dark room. My wife, asleep, would utter some small sound of curiosity before falling silent again. Then I would go to the top drawer of my dresser, the one with all the junk in it. In that drawer I also kept—not a gun, but a heavy carpenter's hammer. One blow could easily kill a man, and I admit that I thought about how to do this, rehearsed it in my mind. How glorious it would be to kill an armed intruder! I pictured the struggle, the two of us tumbling down the stairs. And then the fatal blow, the crunch of the man's skull as I killed him. And then my explanation to the police, with them shaking their heads at the stupidity of the thing. And then the account in the next day's paper. How heroic! And how foolish to be thinking of such things. I could go downstairs with my heroic hammer and be quickly killed by the criminal, who would continue up the stairs to rape my wife and kill my children. Perhaps I should just call 911 and shut the door.

These were my thoughts each time. I never called 911. With the hammer in hand, I would go down the stairs in my underwear and snoop around. Sometimes I yelled "Hey!" into the darkness. Over the years I did this perhaps two dozen times. Nothing ever happened.

. . .

One night, late, with my wife asleep in our bedroom and our children asleep in theirs, I stood and looked out the window at the apartment building behind our house. Directly across from the window I could see a naked woman of about twenty lying on her bed, legs up. Another woman, large and dressed somewhat officiously in a white robe, bustled about the room. The women talked, I could see. Then the large woman knelt down and put her mouth between the other woman's legs. This went on for a minute or two, and then the large woman rose and turned out the light.

. . .

Each morning, before the small washbasin adjoining the bedroom, I shaved with an electric razor, washing the whiskers down the sink afterward. Often my daughter would watch, fascinated, and I would ask her if she would like to shave too, and she would squeal excitedly and run away.

. . .

My wife piled her books and magazines next to her side of the bed. She read voraciously, as they say, but not sequentially. Bits of this or that. Jane Smiley. *The Silence of the Lambs.* A biography of Tolstoy. *Vanity Fair.* Salman Rushdie. Strange accounts of sixteenth-century saints. John Irving. Anything. She loved to read in bed after the children were asleep. In time she purchased a cunning little light that attached to the top of her book. When I got in bed she would say that she would just read a little longer, and I knew that the first of any seductions that evening would be away from the book.

. . .

Most nights the children padded into the bedroom and climbed aloft into the land of Mom and Dad. Sometimes they would sleepwalk their way in, burbling sweet incoherencies, like happy drunks. Other times they ran fiercely through the dark, as if late for an appointment. This got out of hand and soon we had one or two children in the bed at all hours of the night. Inevitably they settled in the valley between my wife and me; we were then forced to the outer perimeters of the mattress, where we would balance precariously on the edge. I myself suffered a number of dreams in which I accidentally plunged off cliffs, tops of buildings, lighthouses. The children, meanwhile, had a propensity to lay crossways, to flail their feet grumpily, to pull the covers, to fart unconsciously. I was kicked any number of times in the face, stomach, and testicles. Some nights they peacefully wet our bed. In time, when the children arrived in the night, I would get up, wish them all a good night (generously or bitterly, depending upon the projected number of hours of sleep), and then trudge up the stairs to the guest bedroom. If we had guests, I would trudge downstairs to the couch. Often I slept quite well.

. . .

I began to spend a little more money on clothes. To have a box of laundered shirts on my bedroom dresser, from which I could choose before going to work, was a small but keen satisfaction.

. . .

During this time my wife and I fought, as is usual and even strangely comforting. Typically we were able to be mad at each other for only about twenty minutes before the conversation devolved into a brilliant exposition of how tired we were, how sick of working all the time, the relentlessness of caring for children, and so on. We had these arguments in the living room, never in the bedroom.

. . .

The bedroom was actually a set of compartmentalized spaces. My spaces were my dresser, my closet, and wherever I had thrown my shoes. (How odd that I communed with the bed and dresser every day and almost never looked *deeply* into my closet, not six feet away.) My wife's spaces were more numerous, and included her dresser, which was larger, her closet, her mountain of books, and a large chest that sat at the foot of the bed. I didn't know what was in this chest, just as I didn't know what, exactly, was in my wife's dresser. On the other hand, she knew exactly what was in my mine.

. . .

It was while sitting in the bedroom, phone against my ear, that I listened to my father describe the condition of his prostate, and what the surgeon would do.

. . .

In the summer I opened the bedroom windows, and one July, from the apartment house in the back, we could hear a child weeping each night at the same time. He cried out for his mother, for water—for love, really. Each night as he lay in bed. Then, as the evening wore on, after he had cried himself to sleep, we could hear his parents arguing in their bedroom from the next window, arguing horribly. Her voice was plaintive, beseeching, apologetic. His sounded sadistic. He may have been hitting her, though it was hard to tell.

. . .

Occasionally I looked in my closet and wondered why in the world I kept clothes that I never wore. Ghastly neckties, pants laughable for their obsolete waistlines. And the shoes I was married in, worn twice, to my own wedding and to my grandmother's funeral: black, heavy, traditional, grim. Each time blisters. You had to be serious in these shoes; the pain precluded laughter and forgetting. Somehow it seemed appropriate to have a pair of formal, excruciating shoes around, and I never got rid of them.

. . .

It was in the bedroom, on the bed, that I contemplated what had just happened to me. Walking home late at night, three men had jumped me and pressed a gun into my left shoulder. My reflexive impulse had been to piss in my pants. "Don't let it be a homicide," the tallest had warned. I didn't. I gave them everything I had—my money and watch and even a bag of old baby clothes I was carrying. The three of them took these things, took the clothes my children had worn, and fled into the dark.

In the bedroom, I again inspected the ceiling cracks, which were getting worse. I looked for a pattern, but couldn't see one.

. . .

From time to time I observed my wife and thought, "She's aging." And when I looked in the full-length mirror screwed to the inside of her closet door, I saw that I was aging too—and maybe faster. My wife, I realized, would age like a beautiful wooden sailboat—signs of wear, but all the lines intact. My own aging pattern resembled a mud slide in slow motion. In the mirror I would inspect the gray hairs, pull out a few, and think myself ridiculous. For a while I did push-ups on the Indian rug before my morning shower, but eventually I gave it up.

. . .

In the bedroom we watched the collapse of the Soviet Union, the Los Angeles riots, Bush debating Clinton, Nancy Kerrigan skating against Tonya Harding, O. J. Simpson's famous ride in the white Ford Bronco, the nerve gas in Tokyo's subways, the Oklahoma bombing. And while my children were in the bath, I laughed at *The Simpsons,* a show my wife found idiotic. In the mornings, sitting on the bed, our children watched *Shining-Time Station,* which featured a magical train conductor played by Ringo Starr. The conversion of a Beatle into an actor on a children's show seemed the final bizarre proof that we were not locked in time, all was moving always, I was aging, my children growing, the twentieth century almost done.

. . .

One winter our children kept getting sick, and finally my wife put the following items next to the bed: spare pajamas, a device that measures body temperature by being inserted into an ear, a towel for the vomit, and a glass of Gatorade, which the pediatrician had said was the only thing you should give a child who is vomiting regularly. In the worst incident our son vomited perhaps ten times in an hour, and my wife sat over him as he lay wan and feverish on our bed. "What if he's *really* sick?" she asked. I reminded her that the emergency room of our local hospital was really not the place to take a sick child. He would wait for hours under harsh lights and get minimal treatment. We stared at each other. All I could think of was the fact that my son had my father's middle name and my father had prostate cancer. "He's sleeping," my wife said. We watched him breathe. There was a bubble of spit on his lip. In the morning he was okay.

. . .

The new bed is huge. King-size, made of cherry, ordered from a lifestyle catalogue. The cost? I didn't care how much it cost, I was tired of a small bed. I was fucking tired of it. The mattresses, also huge, came from DIAL-A-MATTRES. ("Leave off the last S for savings!") Two Mexican men dragged them up the stairs and my wife tipped them ten bucks each, the same amount that our first bed cost. I assembled the bed while our children scribbled on the cardboard packing boxes. The bed is *gigantic.* Now the children come into the bedroom at night or in the morning and there is enough room for everybody. As I drift upward toward consciousness, our daughter grabs my hands and demands to be given arithmetic questions that require counting fingers. After breakfast my children and I return to the bed, where I am commanded to invent new games—involving hidden socks, caves made of blankets, a witch puppet, imaginary bugs, lost stuffed animals, junkyards of matchbox cars. The newness of the bed contrasts with the wear that the room is taking. My wife and I talk sometimes about getting the plaster fixed and having the room painted, but at heart we don't care that much. There is too much else to do.

· · ·

At any given moment the contents of the wastebasket in the bedroom might contain paper bands from laundered shirts, crayons somebody has stepped on, hair from my wife's hairbrush, old gum, part of *The New York Times,* various bits of colored paper that our son has cut up, a broken toy. The dangerous stuff in my top drawer—the pins, the bits of plastic—I've thrown away. The kids are talking about computers now.

· · ·

There will come a time, of course, when we will leave our bedroom. We will move, and the big bed will be dismantled and movers will take the mattress and box springs down the stairs. The photos on the mantel and the knickknacks on the dresser will have been packed away, along with the rug from India and the framed Quaker wedding certificate. I dread such a day, because it will mean either that calamity has befallen us or that a lot of time, *our time,* is gone. The bedroom will be empty again, quiet again, until someone else stands there, looking at the windows and walls and floor, mindful perhaps that the last occupants, my wife and children and me, were only passing through.

# JANE SMILEY

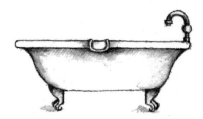

When I lived in Iceland, I had no qualms of conscience at all. There was plenty of rain, and the bathwater bubbled up from the ground already heated to the perfect temperature, so whatever compromises had to be made in terms of bathroom aesthetics—there's never much you can do in a college dorm—were repaid by simple abundance. I came to think of all the hydrothermal resources of Iceland as just so many baths waiting to happen.

I justified my three and sometimes four baths a day by saying (to myself, because no one ever asked) that it was dark (twenty-two hours a day), I was lonely, there wasn't much else to do, but really, I don't think I've ever seen a tub of warm (105–107 Fahrenheit degrees), sparkling, clear water that I didn't want to get into.

The best time to take a bath is before bed. The faintest hint of steam rising off the still surface, a good strong light shining down from the overhead fixture—no mysteries here, the mysteries are in the book I've brought with me to the shore of the tub, some place to rest my drink and my snack and the telephone. The bath is deep—my preferred tub is by Kohler, called "the Greek." After looking at it (okay, transfixed) for a few seconds, I step in, get down, stretch out. The Greek is only four feet long, but the spillover drain is thirty inches above the floor of the tub. With the tub full, I am covered almost to the shoulders, almost to the angles of my bent knees. Getting in does for me what an old cigarette-smoking friend of mine once told me that the first puff of her morning cigarette did for her—it assuages the desire to get in. That's enough. It doesn't have to do any more. I hear some people bathe to get clean, but I bathe so often that cleanliness isn't the primary issue.

You have to give a lot of thought to the floor of the bathroom. Builders have irresponsibly, in my opinion, given in to "master bath syndrome." The first symptom of master bath syndrome is carpeting in the bathroom, which is only one degree less distasteful than carpeting in the kitchen. There's no telling what might slop into bathroom carpeting. Shampoo, conditioner, soapy water, makeup, Dippity-Do and Minipoo. Feces, urine, vomit. Once I was awaiting the arrival of an older, male, and somewhat intimidating poet and novelist. Some twenty minutes before he was due, my daughter staggered into the bathroom with a groan, and I found her there, coiled over the stool, vomiting. I murmured comforting phrases and held her forehead with one hand and her hair, twisted out of her face, with the other. She heaved and heaved. I was incredibly sympathetic, but it was no use. Witnessing her, I felt my own dinner come up, and I had to turn and vomit into the sink. Just then I heard the front door open, and my husband say to the visitor, "I don't know where Jane is. She ought to be down any minute." So, no carpet in the bathroom. But tiles are slippery (the bathroom is the most dangerous room), wood flooring rots, and vinyl sheeting tends to curl up. My favorite floor is composed of those little hexagonal white tiles they used to use in the thirties. They have enough surface to be gripped by wet toes, but they protect the underflooring against water, and you can clean them in a few minutes with a mop and a bucket (no vacuum cleaners in the wettest room in the house). Sybarites can buy some fluffy rugs, which are easily pushed aside when the bathroom is required to receive an accident.

Once I ran away from my boyfriend to a hotel. I wouldn't let my friends tell him where I was, and between baths I made calls to those in the know to find out what his reaction was and how it was progressing. There were some strains in our relationship, but mostly I thought that running away was a dramatically artistic thing to do. I planned to work every moment on a passionately intense but enigmatic story I was writing about my sexual and emotional history. I ended up taking ten baths in thirty-six hours before I got bored and went home. That was the only time I took so many baths that I didn't want to take any more. If communications technology had developed then to where it is now, I would have been able to take the phone with me to the bathroom, and my ten baths might have become one very long one. I wasn't hungry. I couldn't sleep. Taking a bath and talking on the phone fulfilled all of my physical needs, as they have so many times since.

A bathroom needs at least one good window, preferably two or more, including a skylight. And none of that frosted glass. A wide window that runs along the length of the bathtub and gives out on a view of Magen's Bay on the island of Saint Thomas, and the islands beyond where they rise into the rose and indigo morning sky out of the velvety aquamarine and purple sea, is ideal. But from the bathtub, any landscape, even the twisted branches of winter trees in the backyard, is worth contemplating. The contrast between the naked, comfortable, half-floating self and the world outside is always reassuring. Should sleet, driving directly from Canada, be slashing at the skylight as well, then the bather has the choice of enjoying the sound effects (a delicious little shiver) or drowning them out by lifting her toe to the faucet handle and introducing more hot water into the tub.

I love bathing in the middle of the day, when everyone else is at work or school. Right after lunch is a good time, and you can keep working if your work involves reading. A midday bath is better still if it's winter, and you've been out in a cold wind. Let's say the fields are covered with ice but the roads are thawed enough for riding. The only problem is the thirty-mile-per-hour wind blowing directly from the west. Every circuit of a mile-square section must take your face into the wind for at least ten bitter minutes. The sun is pale, and the wind finds the weave in your layers of clothing and whistles through. The horse bucks and pulls and shakes his head, eager for the protection of the barn. By the time you're driving home in the car, your bones are so cold that in spite of the car's heater, you're shivering more when you walk into the house than you were when you left the barn. Now is when the liquid warmth of a bath is thoroughly deserved perfection.

It's amazing to contemplate, but I lived without my own source of hot water for some four years in the early seventies. I had enough money to eat and sleep, but I scrounged for baths. Often, at the houses of friends, when everyone was settling down after dinner for a little conversation, I would say, "Would you mind if I took a bath?" Usually, even people I didn't know very well were startled enough to say "No, go ahead." I hitchhiked through Europe with my first husband, and baths were at a premium. In our archaeological phase, in Winchester, England, the common bathroom had a nice old claw-footed tub, but owing to pressure on the hot water supply, you had to choose your time of day very carefully. In addition, friends we made, true archaeologists who lived in a tent outside the house, owned their own trowels, and subsisted on one pound sterling per week, frequently expressed contempt for another member of the dig, who, they said, was "scrubbing her skin off" with frequent bathing. The acme of our friends' summer was the four days they spent, him holding her upside down by the feet, her removing, trowel by trowel, the contents of a medieval tanner's pit. The contents were known as coprolites. In the Middle Ages, tanners cured leather with animal manure. During these four days, both of our friends felt that bathing would be a waste of time and elected to wait until the excitement was over. This was my first encounter with anti-bath sentiment, and I kept my own baths something of a secret.

Finding good bathing was a hit-or-miss proposition through-

out Europe, at least on the frugal budget we could afford. The
bright spots were the private bathroom we were given at the
youth hostel in Arles, France, which was attached to the private
bedroom we got because we were married, and the bathtub in
our tiny apartment over a bakery in the town of Rethymnon on
the island of Crete. Nightmares abounded. In Bath, England,
once, I thought I'd found solace—the bathtub was big and there
was plenty of hot water, but when I slid down into the water, I
realized that the owner of the bed-and-breakfast had forgotten
to rinse away the abrasive cleaner he'd used on the porcelain, and
by sliding down, I had incorporated it into my dermis. In Paris,
we searched an entire cold and rainy morning for public baths
without finding them, and had to take consolation in a couple
of bowls of *soupe à l'oignon gratinée.*

I always thought I wanted a Jacuzzi in the bathroom. Most
tubs do come in a whirlpool version, and many master baths, especially those with giant master-and-mistress-closet-with-auto-
matic-light facilities, have them. I was disabused of my Jacuzzi
fantasies, however, when my book publisher put me up in the
penthouse suite of a small hotel off Picadilly in London. I
Jacuzzied every spare moment, but in the end, I wasn't woman
enough to withstand the pounding. In the first place, the splash-
ing water made it impossible to read my book, and in the second
place, the jet-powered heat destroyed the very peace that I
sought getting into the bathtub. I emerged over-stimulated but
under-conscious. So, no whirlpool in our bathroom. Still water
cleans deep.

Not everyone has his or her most intimate bathroom relationship with the tub. My sixteen-year-old daughter, for exam-

ple, enjoys the tub, but is far closer to the sink, above which, of course, hangs the mirror. I think of sink-people as face-oriented rather than body-oriented. They take good care of their complexions, floss regularly, pluck their eyebrows, are careful to blend liquid foundation smoothly into their necks, and wear contact lenses. The sink is below them, entirely useful, drain closed, ready to receive anything that drops. They lean over the sink, or sit on it, closer and closer to the mirror. They put their feet in the sink in order to shave their legs. Some people even prefer to wash their hair in the sink. And they think that water from the sink faucet is more potable than water from the tub faucet.

Master bath types love the double sink. They drop "his" sink and "her" sink into acres of countertop as if that's going to solve every problem, but somehow a pedestal sink with a ring of make-up containers balanced around the edge is more appealing, more like a work in progress than a mess. Too much countertop collects things, not only makeup bottles and half-empty samples of shampoo and old razors (danger expresses itself in the bathroom every time you turn around) and dirty towels and needlepoint covers for Kleenex boxes, but also decorative touches, like vases of Italian glass flowers that need to be dusted petal by petal as well as hair and dabs of toothpaste and bits of soap and sand from the beach and small toys and candy wrappers wadded into tiny balls. Too much countertop is a natural magnet. And too much countertop is an excuse for too much mirror.

The main reason for a mirror in the bathroom is to silver the ambient light and thereby lift the spirit. Twenty-four inches wide by thirty inches tall is abundant to the task. Any more mirror, and you end up taking window space. Too much mirror is hard to keep clean and bright. And too much mirror invites two or more people to think they can use the bathroom at the same time, which entirely defeats the larger purpose of the bathroom.

Of course there are those inner-directed types whose most profound relationship is with the stool. I am not one of them, but I feel they should be fully accommodated. A shelf is good, stacked with a few back issues of *Bon Appétit,* the *People* magazine special issue about Jacqueline Kennedy Onassis, a volume of short stories by Dorothy Parker, and some catalogues. I envied a stool once that had a frontal view over the cliff face of the back nine in the valley at River Place, in Austin, Texas, as well as the hill country beyond. The fairways meandered narrowly through the rattlesnake and scorpion infested scrub, a green pattern of a journey reminiscent of a Japanese scroll painting unrolled and seen from afar. I thought it was a bold spot for a builder to place a big window, a bold spot for a self-confident golfer, but the house attached to it was out of my price range.

Choosing the right stool for the bathroom is more complicated than you think it's going to be. A good water-conserving model in a large family can save enough water every seven flushes to afford Mom an extra bath each day. I like the Swedish Ifo, which substitutes a jet of water pressure from above for sucking from below. Its two parts also have a flowerlike, sculptural look, aesthetically pleasing if that's what you have to contemplate from a reclining position in the bathtub.

It may be that shower takers and tub bathers are separate breeds, like cat lovers and dog lovers, but I prefer both. That sluicing feeling should have its place in every life. The shower head, though, should be at least six and a half feet high, and the water pressure strong enough to blast away thought. In regions where the water contains ten to twenty grains of calcium, the shower should have a direct relationship with a water softener. It took me years to realize that that dry feeling my skin had after every shower came as a result of alkaline mineral deposits actually soaking up the moisture in my skin. And the water hitting my face was in effect partly rock. After we installed the water softener, the shower did soften.

Mostly I shower in the morning. A bath in the morning seems like a needless brake on the day, not to mention an act of aggression against the other bathroom users, but from time to time, after a feverish night of flu, half sleeping, half waking, intermittently shivering and sweating into the bunched and creased bedclothes, never really dreaming, but always whirring with partly comprehended imaginings, I want to subside into a hot bath more than anything. It doesn't necessarily make me feel better, but it does make me feel organized. What my daughter prefers is to throw her steaming body across the cool white bathroom floor. The bathroom is the most forgiving place for illness. It's the only place in the house where you can bleed in peace.

I come from a one-bathroom family, and have progressed only as far as one and a half baths in my adult life. During my mother's second marriage, there was an interval of five bathrooms for eight residents, but the old habit of walking in and out of the bathroom and only maybe sometimes remembering to knock was too ingrained to break. The one-bathroom life isn't all bad. It develops the habit of sharing scarcity, makes the achievement of privacy a matter of time as well as of space, gives family members ease and familiarity with one another's bodies, and encourages good manners, as crowded conditions always do.

My children ought to fit into dormitory life quite comfortably. I've spent plenty of bathtub hours drilling my daughters in French verbs, listening to them read compositions aloud, fielding requests, and threatening that if I have to get out of the bathtub in order to find the lost object, I will be really angry. Private bathrooms are not the first requirement of our dream house, but it's true that when we check into a hotel suite, we scatter to the three or four bathrooms first thing, just to try them out.

I read about a woman with twenty-one children once. The bathroom was her favorite room in the house. Mine, too. Alone and naked in the bathroom, sunk in the life of the body, the life of the face, the inner life. The tiny tiles are smooth and cool against the soles of your feet. The light is bright, shined up by the mirror. Your skin is warm enough and cool enough. The sounds of the house are muffled or, better still, lost in the always therapeutic sound of water running. Your stuff is spread all over the place, claiming the bathroom, temporarily, as your own space. The book. The glass of orange juice. The short stack of Fig Newtons. The clean towels, clean floors, clean basins, clean mirror, and clean windows. If you've cleaned them yourself, then this is your chance to enjoy them. The air is moist. Vapory fragrances commingle. The color palette of your little world here is mostly neutral—whites or creams—with more vivid accents of towels, pictures, and rugs enlivening the eye here and there. You are Self Centered, as is your perfect right in the bathroom. This is the core of the house, the safest place for all its dangers, the spot where, if a tornado came and you didn't have a basement, you'd take refuge. Tornado or no tornado, you already do take refuge here, in the eternal now of the physical life.

# ESMERALDA SANTIAGO

A t first, there was a rough pole debarked and smoothed, nailed to the north and east walls of our one-room house so that it made the base of a triangle. From the pole dangled three metal hangers and from them, my mother's clothes: one flowered dress for celebrations, one sky blue with white piping for official visits, and the black one necessary for solemn occasions. She tied a string to two more nails in front of the pole, and from it hung a faded sheet that protected her clothes from dust and prying eyes. The triangle formed by the two walls and stretched sheet was a world away from my parents, my four sisters, and two brothers. Bony spine wedged into the corner, I sat under Mami's dresses for hours, knees folded up to my chin, arms wrapped around my legs, eyes closed, waiting for something to happen.

By then, Papi had covered the flattened earth floor with wood. In the areas where our bare feet walked, the planks were smooth and shiny, but under the beds, and in the corner under my mother's city clothes, the floor was rough and scratchy. Often, splinters caught my panties, so that Mami had to mend them or, to judge by her complaints and reproaches, buy me more than I was entitled to.

But no matter how much she threatened, I slipped into the percha whenever I needed to be alone. It became my private refuge where, it seemed, even Mami felt as if she were intruding when she went to get her dresses for a baptism, a visit to the doctor, or a funeral.

I papered the walls of the percha with newspaper clippings of cars wrapped around trees, bloody sheets with the bumpy outline of corpses in bizarre positions, an ominously empty electric chair. My dark corner commemorated the abstract black-and-white violence of a world far from my rural Puerto Rican barrio. It was the violence of drunken brawls in street corner bars, of crimes of passion in stacked apartments in San Juan, of bank robberies in New York and gang violence in Chicago.

When I sat under Mami's three dresses, in the midst of gore, I didn't think about these things. I was a child, and didn't have to deal with any of it just yet. But the clippings introduced me to a wild, big place beyond the entrance to the barrio, a place of horror and fear and danger.

One day, a rickety truck sputtered into our yard, and Papi and his friend Dima unloaded a present for Mami. It was a wardrobe, one side of which had four deep drawers, the other a tall narrow cabinet for clothes. Mami was delighted. The four drawers held all the clothes for us seven children. The tall cabinet was for Mami's three dresses and, once we started school, the uniforms she ironed for us every morning.

"I don't want you in the closet," she told me when I tried to wedge into it as I used to do in the percha.

"It's too narrow anyway," I replied sullenly. Even with my shoulders hunched, the walls of the wardrobe crushed my ribs into my chest, making it hard to breathe. Mami took down the percha, and I had to find another place to hide.

There were always lengths of splintery lumber and jagged sheets of corrugated steel lying around our yard, the debris from my father's improvement projects. I collected whatever wasn't nailed to anything else, and dragged it to a spot between two mango trees. I used only the rusty nails Papi saved in a jar, some of which I had to straighten by banging them with Papi's best hammer against a flat rock. My sisters and brothers watched and asked what I was up to, but I scared them off with threats. They circled my creation, whining and complaining. When they told Mami I wouldn't let them play with me, she warned them to leave me alone. That was one advantage of being the eldest. Sometimes, Mami took my side.

My house was tall enough for me to enter upright, but I had to get on my knees to stay inside for any length of time, since, given the nature of the found materials it was built from, the corner posts were all different sizes, so that the roof pitched sharply to one side. Mami gave me scraps of fabric to string curtains in the openings I had left for windows, and for the door. I papered the walls with new soft-focus images of accident and murder scenes, and with painstakingly copied poems from my schoolbooks. The dirt floor I swept clean, and against the sloping corner I built a percha, from which I hung three dresses fashioned from Papi's newspaper. They were not at all like Mami's dresses. I drew and cut out three gowns, shaped with the curves and cleavage of the movie stars pictured in the gossip columns. I painted them in primary colors, using the small pots of tempera the Three Magi had left me in gratitude for the fresh grass and water I had left for their camels.

The stiff gowns curled into themselves, the way I had to in Mami's wardrobe, so I kept replacing them with newly fashioned ones, each more elaborate and colorful than the last, not a single dark one among them because, as a child, I was not expected to wear black to funerals.

I sat in my little house, curtains drawn shut, and listened to my sisters and brothers chase one another in the yard, or to Mami yelling at them to stop doing this or that, or to my father banging nails into walls. I filled the percha with the colorful, curvy dresses I imagined rich women wore, and dreamed of someday having a closet full of just such dresses to choose from.

Every year, on the last day of school, there was an assembly for those of us smart enough to pass from one grade to the next. The girls were expected to wear white dresses, and the boys long pants with a white shirt and tie. Three months before the ceremony, Mami began making the dresses that I and my two younger sisters would wear. The others were not old enough to be in school, but Norma, Delsa, and I got a brand-new dress each summer for the end of school, and, after that, we wore them to family gatherings and other special events.

I loved the dresses Mami made, with bows, ribbons, lace,

scalloped collars, embroidered sleeves. But I hated the starched crinolines she made us wear to show off her carefully fashioned skirts. They were scratchy and hot. When I sat down, they popped up in front, and if I squished them down, they spread to the side, taking up the space reserved for the kids on either side of me. But Mami insisted that the dresses did not look good without cancans. I wore a miserable expression on my face throughout the ceremony, walked in small steps to minimize the scratching on my thighs, and held my arms stiff against the fluffy skirts so they wouldn't rise up and suffocate me when I sat down.

In the percha of my little house, the paper dresses began to look like those the flappers wore in the twenties. Straight and limp and non-threatening.

Because Mami couldn't get along with Papi in the country, we moved to Santurce. In our new house, rising on stilts over a fetid lagoon, there was no percha, no wardrobe, no closet. We folded our belongings into a dresser warped by moisture and poor workmanship.

We lived in one room. The sink where we washed our faces, brushed our teeth, and did the dishes was a metal-lined platform outside the back window with holes punched at the bottom for the water to drain into the lagoon. A sill cock for fresh water sprouted off one side, at the end of a long tube suspended over the black lagoon by nails shaped into loops, or tied with rope to the docks leading to the houses rising over the water where digested and undigested food floated in infinite variety. It was in El Mangle that I discovered we were poor, for surely no one who wasn't poor would live over their own filth.

I often thought of running away, back to Macún and my little house under the mango trees. But I didn't have the courage.

When Papi and Mami reconciled, we moved once more, to another house in Santurce, this one behind a bar, where nightly brawls kept us awake. Mornings, on our way to school, we skipped over the dark stains left by drunken men who urinated and retched against the side of the house. Papi built a percha covered with a flowered sheet, and in it Mami put her three dresses, and Papi's shirts, and our uniforms, freshly pressed so that we looked clean and crisp, like children from the neighborhoods the customers of the bar behind which we lived had escaped.

I lost my desire for small spaces in Santurce. I longed for open fields that smelled of newly turned earth.

When we moved to another rural barrio, I got my own room and, rather than have a percha, I hung my uniform and party dress on the walls, displayed like trophies on hangers covered with crochet stitches. I liked looking at what I owned: two blouses and one skirt for school, a white-and-blue party dress, loafers for school and shiny patent leather shoes for special occasions. My underwear I folded in a basket, but Mami made me put it under the bed because underwear, she said, should not be displayed for everyone to see.

And then, we moved again, this time away from Puerto Rico, to New York. Papi didn't come with us here, either. He stayed and started a new life with a whole other family. He built a house for them, and I think it had closets, but I'm not sure because I was never in it. I didn't talk to him for years because I was afraid of hearing happiness in his voice.

In Brooklyn, Mami carefully examined the closets in the

apartments we moved to approximately every six months. There were always empty, twisted metal hangers in those closets, as if the previous residents wished to make a statement about their lives. We threw those hangers out, even though, had they been straightened, they could have been useful.

When we moved on, Mami insisted we leave the apartments spotless, so that the new tenants wouldn't get a bad impression of Puerto Ricans. We scrubbed floors and walls, spackled holes, washed windows. We emptied out the closets, including our rusty and bent wire hangers. By then we were a family of eleven children headed by a single mother. But when we moved, we left no trace that we had ever lived there. In our new apartments, we'd have to clean and scrub all over again because the previous owners were not as concerned with appearances as Mami was.

One year we were able to rent a whole house. A small room off the kitchen, which had served as a pantry, became mine. It was just large enough for a bed and the bright yellow desk I chose at the used-furniture store. The door that led into the kitchen from my room had glass panes, which I covered with a lace curtain. There was a window at the other end of the room, and next to it, a narrow dark cupboard from which I removed the shelves. I nailed a pole across it and, for the first time, had my very own closet.

But I had a funny feeling about that cupboard. A strange smell wafted from the floor, which was covered with old linoleum that seemed pasted to the boards underneath. Mami said a mouse might have died under there and that the smell would go away in a few days.

The thought of carcasses rotting in my room was not comforting. Before long, I was convinced that something lived there, only it was bigger, uglier, and more malevolent than a dead New York City mouse. Noises from the closet kept me awake at night. I felt a presence whenever I opened the door, but it seemed as if whatever was inside waited to be invited out.

If I had told Mami, who didn't believe in the supernatural, she might have reassigned the room to one of my less superstitious sisters or brothers. So I kept quiet and tried to handle the situation on my own. At the library, I looked up ways to exorcise rooms of unwanted spirits. I burned candles and incense. I twisted several heads of garlic into a wreath and hung it inside the closet, hoping it would discourage whatever vampire-like creature lived inside. In case the creature believed in God, I also hung a rosary and the Spanish and English "Our Father." It didn't work. Sometimes, I opened the closet to put something in or take something out, and felt as if a hand waited to grab mine and pull me in there.

By this time I was nineteen, a high school graduate with a job as a mail clerk and a full-course load at a community college. I was, I thought, a mature young woman with responsibilities, who ought not to be afraid of a closet. But my fear of losing the privilege of being the only one of the eleven sisters and brothers to have her own room kept me from going public.

One Saturday, I left the house early to take a test. While I was out, my grandmother, who lived with us, put away clothes she'd washed for me in my closet, forgetting to close the door when she was done. When I returned that afternoon, exhausted and vulnerable, I threw my books on the desk and myself on the narrow bed. The closet was across the desk, which was between the bed and the window. Because I slept facing the curtained door, the closet was behind and to my left.

I dozed and almost instantly felt a blast of cold, putrid air, and then a large reddish-brown, furry something, with very bad breath, slipped out of the closet and quietly walked toward me. It walked on two feet. It had the face of an evil collie, with wild eyes, long fangs, and a lolling tongue that I knew was capable of speech. It growled softly, intimately. I lay stiff and quiet, wishing to wake up, now, wake up now, wake up now, wake up, wake up. The creature jumped on me and its claws ripped into my belly and thighs. I woke up with my nails embedded in the flesh around my navel. The outside of my thighs was marked with deep red welts from my knees to my hips.

I ran out of the room screaming, and found my grandmother stewing beef for that night's supper. Sobbing hysterically, I explained what had happened, and Tata, who believed everything, came into the room and began shouting into the closet. It was a language I'd never heard, with many ings, wangas, and pentús. She slammed the closet door shut, clapped her hands three times, and went back to her beef stew.

I searched my bed for reddish-brown hair, but couldn't find any. Tata came back with some Vick's VapoRub, which she smeared on the scratches on my thighs and belly, rubbing up and down, up and down, until my entire body felt warm and soothed. Then she made me lie on the bed again, but this time, she said I should sleep facing the closet door, because the creature would not come out if it knew I was watching for it.

"Those creatures," she said, "feed on fear, so don't let them surprise you. Let them know you know what they're up to." She took down the heads of garlic, the rosary, and the two prayers. "If you try to protect yourself, they'll know you're scared."

"But I am scared," I said.

"Of course you are, but they don't have to know it. What you do," she said, sitting on the edge of the bed, "is tell the creature all the brave things you have done. That will make it afraid of you."

Tata was an alcoholic, so I never considered her the most reliable source of information. But the garlic and prayers hadn't worked.

Every night, before going to sleep, I stood in front of the closet door, opened it ajar, and whispered, "I'm not afraid of you. Today I was alone in the subway station, and a big man came toward me like he was going to mug me and I just looked him in the eye and smiled."

On the way home every night I reviewed my day, looking for acts of bravery that would scare a collie-like reddish brown creature with a lolling tongue capable of speech.

"A kid on a bicycle rode past me, and as he passed, he stuck his hand out and touched my breast. I chased him and pushed him off the bike and kicked him where it hurts."

I felt ridiculous. I was nineteen, a college student, a worker, and every night I stood at my closet door boasting into the dark. But within days the closet seemed less ominous, the foul smell dissipated, and I no longer felt a frightening presence every time I opened the door.

That summer I fell in love. I was not allowed to date, so I got engaged. Jan proposed after I explained that's the only way Mami would let me go out with him. We had known each other one day.

The next Sunday, he came to the house bearing a box of

chocolate-covered cherries and a bunch of roses. He was German, and knew the Old World way of doing things, so he gal-
lantly asked my mother for my hand. She gave it to him, and he
drove me to the beach in his Porsche.

Mami was very impressed with Jan, and agreed that I didn't
have to give her an allowance from my salary, since I would be
needing every penny for the splashy wedding she was organizing.

I bought *Bride's* magazine, and learned about trousseaus. "I
need silk teddies," I said to Mami, and she let me squander my
money on the fanciest underwear and nightclothes I could afford. My closet began to look like the percha I had built in
Macún, only the shimmery satin slips and nightgowns were real.

But as the summer progressed, I realized I was not in love
with Jan. I was in love with Ben Henry. And then with Hans. And
with Bill and Allan and Tommy. I kept buying fancy clothes, and
dating Jan whenever he was in town, and the other men when
he wasn't. I told myself I was making sure I loved Jan before I
married him, even though I was fairly certain I didn't.

Mami put a down payment on an elaborate wedding gown,
with the curves and cleavage of a movie star. For the reception,
we bought a silk moiré suit with rhinestone buttons. But by then
I had met Çalim. He was Turkish, a year older than Mami, and
wouldn't go along with proposing before dating. I was a little
afraid of him, but the creature in the closet had made me brave.

I met Çalim every day after work, and pretended he didn't
scare me. He challenged me to do things my mother would
never approve of, and before long, I had broken off my engage-
ment to Jan and had forgotten Ben Henry, Hans, Bill, Allan, and
Tommy.

When Çalim asked me to run away with him, I did, bringing with me a small bag with my toothbrush and toothpaste, my hairbrush, several silk teddies and satin nightgowns, and two pairs of shoes. Çalim bought me clothes in subdued colors that he said were elegant. He told me I should not put on makeup, because I didn't need it. He showed me how to wear my hair and how to handle a knife and fork European style. Two weeks after running away with him, I sat in the closet of our fancy apartment in Fort Lauderdale, my bony spine wedged into the corner, under all the stiff clothes he said were elegant, and I cried, listening to him and his Turkish friends laughing and talking and having a good time I was not allowed to share because I was a woman.

For the next five years, I lived with Çalim, retreating into the closet in frustration and fear every time he convinced me that the world outside our apartment was inhospitable and I would not be able to get along in it without him.

"Forget," he said, "your family. They're poor and insignificant and can't do anything for you."

I did not speak to my mother for years, ashamed she would hear the unhappiness in my voice.

I could not answer our telephone, could not have my own friends, could not go out, except to and from work, unless he went with me. He chose my clothes, the television shows we watched, the way we spent the money I made as a bilingual secretary. If I complained, he said I was childish. I thought of running away, but I did not have the courage.

So I applied to college. He didn't think I needed an education, but he was impressed by power. He agreed I shouldn't turn down a scholarship to Harvard.

He found me an apartment walking distance to the college. It was a large studio, with a deep walk-in closet with a mirrored door. I could not escape my reflection as I moved around the apartment. Inside, we hung the clothes he had bought me, tailored, elegant clothes, for my new, elegant life.

Çalim had a job in New York, and I lived in Cambridge, free of his daily presence but not his phone calls. He called precisely at 11:00 P.M., because by then I should have been home, and again at 7:30 A.M. What he feared could happen between 11:00 P.M. and 7:30 A.M., I made sure happened in the daytime hours between.

One day, I realized I hadn't cried in the closet in months. The refined clothes Çalim had chosen for me hung in the deepest part, and were dusted off for formal or solemn occasions, or when Çalim came to visit. The front was filled with gypsy skirts and colorful T-shirts, so that each day felt as if I were celebrating. Mornings, as I chose a red skirt or hot-pink top, I told myself how brave I was to wear such violent colors.

The day Çalim walked out of my life ("You're getting too independent for me," he said), I made reservations to return to Puerto Rico, where Mami had moved the family after I ran away from home.

For the first time in years I spoke to my father, who *was* happy. I had dinner with him and his wife, in the house he had built for her, in which he had raised her children as his own. The closets were jammed with athletic trophies, bridesmaids' dresses in plastic bags, boxes filled with old report cards and photographs. I wondered if they had hidden them there so that I wouldn't feel bad.

I went to Macún, where my mother and siblings had returned, and talked to her as if no one had ever come between us.
We walked to the site of our old house, thirty yards from an
arrow pointing the way to an exit off the recently opened highway into the city. Near the weed-encrusted fence that separated
what remained of Macún from the highway, there was a mound
of wormy wood and jagged metal, the remains of our first home.

A foul smell rose from the ruins, as if something were rotting. I stood atop the mound, my back to what would have been
the northeast wall, awed by how much had happened. Then
Mami and I walked side by side to her house, farther up the road.
It was made of cement, with a tile floor. Each of the four bedrooms had a small, dark closet filled with my sisters' and brothers' school uniforms and party clothes. But in her room she had
a wardrobe with four drawers along the side and a tall narrow
cabinet next to them. It was crammed with dresses she wore only
for solemn occasions, with no room for even the smallest child
to hide in.

# KATHRYN HARRISON

The children are young enough that the passage between our two bedrooms is still umbilical, a door through which I travel nightly, once or twice between midnight and dawn, sometimes more often. Summoned by a cry, impelled by a worry or nightmare of my own, I don't wake fully in the journey from our bed to our son's—nine steps—or our daughter's—fourteen. I kneel beside whichever child I've come to comfort; sometimes I let my cheek rest on the foot of the bed and fall back into my dreams. When I rouse myself, minutes or hours later, I am cold, stiff, confused. The night light, which seems so weak at bedtime that it fails to illuminate the cars and dolls and blocks underfoot, dazzles my just-opened eyes. The entire room is gold and glowing, and I can see each eyelash curled against his cheek, can count the pale freckles on her nose.

Boy and girl, they are still young enough that they share this large room that adjoins our bedroom, the room that, innocent of children, my husband and I imagined would be a library. After all, it has a whole wall of floor-to-ceiling bookcases. When we moved in we had just married, and I unpacked as I had when I was single and childless: books before clothes, before bedding or dishes or records or pictures or toiletries. I transferred novels and poems and essays from their boxes (packed as they had been shelved, alphabetically) directly into the empty cases. At last here was a home with built-in shelves! A fireplace, and furniture inherited from the grandmother who raised me—antique steamer trunks, mahogany chairs and desk, a chaise longue for more desultory study—contributed to our literary aspirations for the space.

Now, only the chaise remains. All but the top four shelves are emptied of grown-up books and filled with toys, picture books, art supplies. I have removed our novels and essays, poems and histories as I have needed to, in response to our children's ability to reach and climb. I carried them upstairs and stacked them, A's and M's and Z's all jumbled together and furred with dust. This was the way in which the room was transformed from library to nursery: book by book, shelf by shelf, chair by chair. I wonder if it is by equally small increments that we become parents, as our children claim another and another sinew of devotion.

The chaise longue harks back to an age of extravagance and leisure. Having begun its career a century ago in my great-grandmother's bedroom in Shanghai, it accompanied her to Nice, and then traveled with my grandmother to London and to Los Angeles. The chaise has always been a bedroom furnishing.

For more than one hundred years, it has resided in bedrooms in a matriarchal line that includes my mother, myself, and now our daughter, Sarah, conceived in the midst of my unpacking our books. Had I considered the history of the chaise, perhaps I might have been forewarned of the true vocation of the room into whose window alcove it settled immediately, unbudgingly; perhaps I might have been warned that while the chaise would not be moving to another room, the books would. Stuffed with goose down, it can easily accommodate one parent and both children and has always been upholstered in velvet: blue originally, a cherry pink during my infancy, and now a regrettable, bilious shade of green. The fabric splits at points of stress and white feathers leak from the rents that I hand stitch, only to have the fabric split open again an inch or two away from my labors. Not one of the hours I have spent in the chaise's weary embrace has been given to silent reading or any other solitary recreation.

Sarah's arrival was followed by that of her crib. Hundred-spindled, made of fruitwood, it displaced two chairs and the desk. When she woke at two or at four and called me to her, I stumbled from our bed to the crib and reached over its tall side. I took her into my arms and took us both into the chaise, where we ultimately fell asleep together, my nipple still in her mouth.

Long before she stopped nursing, before we were weaned from each other and from our crumpled, postprandial naps, Sarah began acquiring *things,* many of them. The baby swing and toy chest nudged the steamer trunks to our living room; a rocking chair replaced the last of its immobile colleagues. Colin and I bought a craft table so small that even carefully folded onto the matching stools, we cannot coax our humped knees under its surface, now covered with sedimentary layers of adhesives and pigment. Long before kindergarten, our daughter became enamored of Play-Doh, paste, poster paint, acrylic paint, glitter paint, oil paint, and Magic Markers. In short order she acquired a glue gun, a glutinous, slippery, shiny gunk called Gak, Silly Putty, plaster of Paris, a machine that employs centrifugal force to splatter paint onto whirling cards, and a little brother—all of which arrivals encouraged the exchange of the mauve Oriental rug for a nearly wall-to-wall Stainmaster III in a practical shade of dark blue.

Three years old, the carpet already wears its history. People who do not have children will give other people's children the sort of gifts their parents never buy, hence the popularity of bachelor uncles and courtesy aunts. Hence the glue gun and Gak. I drew the line at hot paraffin and hid the candle-making kit, but still, we paint and draw and mold and glue a lot—every day—and the more ambitious art projects do leave incidental impressions, stains, gouges. The rocking chair, I noticed recently, has been decorated intentionally, with stickers and wobbly stripes of red and green around its arms and along the side of its seat. It has older scars, of course; this rocker was in my childhood bedroom, and before that, in my mother's. It has been glued and clamped, screwed and reglued by both my grandfather and my husband.

It has to be strong, for in another few years Sarah or her brother, Walker, will discover the joy of "riding" the rocker. If you stand with a foot on each of its arms and tip it back and forth, back and forth, you can achieve a kind of clumsy tightrope effect, albeit without forward process; that was the least of my childhood antics. When I was eight my favorite rainy-day trick was tobogganing down my grandparents' long, carpeted stairs on a tea tray. Once, I jumped off a roof with an open umbrella, à la Mary Poppins; it didn't work: I went down, not up, and sprained my ankle. I haven't told my children any of this, certainly not how I climbed the garden gate and then the rain gutter and used the long pole of the leaf net to vault from the roof of my grandparents' house into their swimming pool. I did that because of, not in spite of, its dangers; but our children, I like to think, have more sense than I did. Even now, I was the first to jump up and down on the mattress of the master bedroom's new king-size bed.

"Are you supposed to be doing that?" Sarah said.


The baby swing and changing table, the crib and the walker are gone now, and each of the children has what is called a "youth" bed, smaller than a twin and closer to the floor. At five, Sarah is nearly too large for hers, but she's not ready to part with it yet. She hated to lose its predecessor, the crib, which we tactfully dismantled long before her brother's arrival, and only after we had put together her new little bed with its shiny, red-enameled frame. We were careful to allow a full six months between Sarah's moving out of the crib and Walker's moving in, careful that she never felt she was forced to pass her bed directly along to another baby, but still Sarah wept when its polished wood back and foot and sides were carried from the room. Walker, for whom a crib was never better than an inadequately disguised cage, clapped at its second dismantling. He bounced on his version of the little bed, the same as Sarah's but enameled in blue. "Just like Rah-rah, just like Rah-rah!" he rejoiced. Before Walker mastered sibilance, Sarah's exuberant nature made "Rah-rah" a good nickname for his sister.

Between the two little beds is the fireplace, whose flue is permanently shut, bricked up. The empty hearth has become a cubby hole for an appropriately combustible-looking collection of junked toys—Barbie's broken refrigerator and her hot pink range, a fire engine without its wheels, stray blocks, twisted and retwisted pipe cleaners, ravaged coloring books—all trash they cannot bear to discard. Together the objects make a blaze and jumble of color. Presiding disconsolately over the heap is the piñata from the most recent birthday party. A papier-mâché donkey with a festive hide and mane of orange and red and pink tissue paper, he was torn in two, vivisected by preschool greed wielding a broom. Now his head and tail both face in the same direction—out into the bedroom, so we are spared the dispiriting sight of his hollow middle. The mantelpiece above bears another rubble of objects, most of which Sarah hopes to keep out of Walker's reach: stickers, costume jewelry, a collection of tiny plastic horses. He's cleverly kept it a secret that he can stand on the foot of his bed and get what he wants.

Propped in the center of the mantel is an old wall hanging: a wood bas-relief of an inn, including kitchen, dining hall, and bedrooms. Every object and gesture is carved and painted with cunning attention: dinner plates the size of quarters, a butter churn with a three-inch dash, washtubs, rolling pin, crucifix, table and benches, a clock whose hands read a quarter past five, hats hanging on hooks by the door, an accordion, two flowerpots, shotgun, and stove. My grandfather, who was apprenticed in 1904 to a cabinetmaker in Berlin (he was fourteen), acquired the hanging, which was made in Germany's Black Forest. It used to contain a working music box, and just under the eaves projects a brass key that no longer turns. The hidden mechanism, with its rolling, metal-toothed platen and minuscule comb of tines, once played, my grandfather told me, a feeble polka.

As a child, I spent many hours staring at the tavern's tiny furnishings, at once seduced and bewildered by the very nature of bas-relief, neither flat picture nor free sculpture, a dollhouse enduring an uneasy metamorphosis from three dimensions to two. Later, as a young woman, I had too self-conscious an aesthetic to hang it on the wall but couldn't throw or give it away. If I didn't love the object itself, still it seemed that the little tavern held all the hours I had given to it, that within its disconcerting neither-this-nor-that self it kept a little of what I once was: equally ill defined, one thing becoming another. Before we had children, I moved the tavern from closet to basement to guest room and back to closet, never knowing what to do with it, until Sarah and Walker showed me.

"Take it down! I want to look at it up close!" they say. The request is never more avid than when they are ill, and I can remember, exactly, how fever enhanced the little row of frying pans hung over the stove, gilded the flowers painted on cupboard doors the size of my thumbnail. I can remember, in the glaze and glitter of their feverish eyes, but I can no longer *feel* the luxury of benign childhood illness, of recoveries uncompromised by meetings, deadlines, chores.

When I was only a little older than our daughter, the arduous boredom of another bout of tonsillitis once inspired me to climb the shelves of my grandmother's cavernous linen closet, which beckoned, door ajar, from the hall. I got out of bed and began to ascend from beach towels on up through sheets and bath towels and tablecloths. Once I had reached the musty, dizzy, camphor-redolent heights reserved for heavy-weight wool blankets, I could not get down. Fever made the shelves tremble beneath my bare feet, the far-off floor wavered, and I couldn't remember just how I had ascended—undoubtably in the shivery euphoria of a spiking 103, fever climbing with the patient and leaving me in the precarious, confused altitude of 105 and 106. Later that afternoon I had a febrile convulsion, which was blamed on the climb.

So from experience, I know that if not sufficiently entertained, my children will escape the confines of bed; and I supply toys, rescind the TV laws, and bring them from their room into ours. In our family sick children inevitably end up in the parental bed, an indulgence intended to compensate for an ailment serious enough to mandate bed rest: a way of separating horizontal day from night, a chance to command the empire of our tall, king-size bed, at whose foot I prop the tavern.

"Why," Sarah asks, as I asked my grandfather, "are the flames right on the pot?" A tiny black kettle hangs in the kitchen over kindling the size of matchsticks, its underside painted with tongues of red and yellow and orange.

"Because," I say, not finishing the answer any more than my grandfather did, in 1910 they didn't have cellophane for fake fires.

Not only my own childhood is recapitulated in our children's bedroom, their father's is here as well. Along the top shelf of the

bookcase are twenty-nine bottles and nine glass inkwells, anywhere from 90 to 120 years old. Clear, clouded, blue, green,
brown—old enough that none are actually colorless, that even
plain glass has gone a shade of green or blue. Though dug from
old dumps, none are chipped or broken. There are hundreds of
these bottles in our house, most packed away, all of them together
representing thousands of hours of Colin's childhood.

Time continues to possess and confound and mystify the
parents of the children in whose room we linger. It passes, of
course, with a relentlessness familiar to all grown-ups, but never
more than when compared to the clock of childhood, with its
burden of hours to be wasted, a burden compounded by the as
yet misperceived vagaries of hour hands and minute hands and
calendars. Questions of measurement include: When will it be
Christmas, Summer, Friday, My birthday? Dinner? Young children float on an ocean unmarked by adult dates and appoint-
ments. Sarah stands at the front door, dressed to go, whole hours
before a birthday party. Walker looks out the window of the car,
"Are we there yet" uttered while still in our neighborhood. He
cannot imagine that his parents treasure long car rides for their
enforced enclosure, their near idleness. Increasingly, the car is the
only place to talk, for at meals we are drowned out or inter-
rupted; in bed we are too busy and then, abruptly, too exhausted.

But childhood has many hours that must be filled. Is this one
reason for our curiously misguided idealization of it? Waiting for
important phone calls, we read professional journals while riding our exercise bikes. Dinner cooks slowly in the crock pot
while I fold the laundry, catch the lead stories of the 6:30 news,
and police the crayon situation (she takes his reds, he breaks her

blues). How different from the time when we drooped over banisters, loitered limply at the back door, moaned "But I have nothing to do. I'm so, so, so bored."

At ten or twelve, my afternoons were squandered on prank phone calls, conversations with people picked at random from the phone book. I measured the success of these calls by their duration; my objective was to make a chance connection with a stranger, one that could not be dismissed: to engage that stranger for whole minutes, every so often a quarter of an hour or more. Colin dug in old dumps for bottles, unearthing layers of rusted springs, rotted cloth, coins, stoppers, forks, and broken glass. When he found a whole bottle he held it to the light, imagined the hands that dropped it a hundred years before, hands that were buried or burned. Lost. But the bottle was not lost, the bottle was found.

While our children wait to be older, imagining perhaps that grown-up busyness is a measure of their happiness and freedom, Sarah and Walker are amused by Barbies and blocks and crayons and tiny cars, by trains, stuffed animals, picture books, dress-up clothes, beads, stencils, pipe cleaners, fire engines, balls, balloons, putty, puzzles, and puppets. All of these, in every state of disrepair (Madison Avenue Barbie reduced to a gruesome paraplegic, her hair matted into dreadlocks), form a tide that washes over all the surfaces of their room. Beds, tables, chairs, nothing is uncovered, clutter is fierce, the room infrequently tidy. Still, "What a great room!" everyone says when they enter for the first time. The walls are decorated with Babar and Mickey Mouse and Muppets; they are decorated with these lighthearted figures in determined contrast to my own room as a child, with its one print, entitled *In Disgrace,* of a little girl, face to the wall, blue sash drooping, socks rumpled, sad-eyed puppy at her scuffed heels. Flanking this watercolor were two framed prayers by Mary Baker Eddy, the founder of Christian Science. Of a troubling and final nature, each seemed to indicate that I was not long for this world.

As a small child, I was high-spirited, careless, clumsy, and often in "Coventry," my British grandparents' way of saying "doghouse." Even without the solace of canine sympathy, I knew myself to be that painted, rumple-socked girl sprung to life. Who needed to tell me that I was my mother's disgrace? She was pregnant and unmarried the summer after she graduated from high school, and every look she gave me was one of regret. My mother's parents raised me to be all that she was not—responsible and studious and steady—and they decorated my childhood bedroom to exclude the whimsy revealed in photographs of my mother's room, with its three dollhouses and trunks of dress-up clothes. Before I could read, I had a desk, a bookcase, and edifying messages on the wall—none of which helped to keep me out of the trouble I was bound to find.

Sarah was still in the crib when I bought the giant Mickey Mouse decal, cut him out of the vast sheet of adhesive-backed polyurethane, cut out each one of the tide of yellow stars on which he rides, placed them all with care. By design, the room is filled with happy nonsense, and yet our daughter seems already the studious, responsible child I was meant to be. "I'm going to my office," she says of her own art desk, a red and yellow and blue and green one whose surface includes a light box for tracing. Sometimes Sarah traces pictures, more often words, sentences. Her hair falls around her while she works, hunched over in concentration, the light under her carefully moving pencil shining out through the dark strands. "What are you doing?" I ask. "My work," she says.

We redress the hurts of our own childhoods, we do it even with abundant evidence that our efforts rarely matter. Last Christmas, in the guise of Santa Claus, I bought our son an inflatable clown. Three feet tall and weighted with sand at his feet, he is the type of long-suffering companion who, when hit, pops back up. Having struggled under the seen-and-not-heard rule that hopes to cure little girls of untoward zest, I found the clown irresistible. But the only time our son pushes him over is to use him as an inflatable log, a kind of bench. "What's the matter with him?" Walker asks me. "He won't lie down."

"Here," I say. "If you hit him, he pops up again." I demonstrate. Walker gives the clown a casual smack, shrugs. Every once in a while, passing through our children's room, I push the clown over, watch him rise cheerfully, inviting another assault. If I hadn't been overcome by the exigencies of holiday shopping, I would have realized that I wanted to buy the clown for another child, not Walker but a child who exists only in memory, and in her intermittent, ghostly longings.

I find that I come into our children's room when I am alone, anxious. Sarah is in kindergarten, Walker is in nursery school, the house is quiet. I put off work to sit in the chaise or lie on one of their beds that are so short I must curl, knees drawn up, to fit. Sometimes I tidy the room. If I can locate all the pieces of a board game, find both the left and right of Barbie's pair of pink plastic pumps, my worries are somehow lessened by imposing order on chaos, even this happy chaos. By my ability to find something we assumed was lost. I especially like to complete the puzzles, whose pieces are always scattered. Colin's mother has given each of the children a wooden one, featuring a child standing undressed before a closet. Walker's little boy has interchangeable trousers and shirts and pairs of shoes, seven of each, and Sarah's little girl can try on skirts, jackets, dresses, and shoes.

For many months the red cowboy boots have been missing from among the puzzle girl's accessories. One morning I find the piece lodged under a baseboard in our room, and feel a tiny leap of joy: the redemption of recovery. I go to put the piece away, so eager to press it into the empty boot-shaped space that as I cross the threshold from our room to the children's, I almost miss what I am walking over. At my feet is a life-size version of the puzzle I am hoping to complete.

At five, our daughter is just beginning to understand herself as a creature of infinite possibility. We, her parents, each year let go of things we will likely never do, another trip we may not make, another sport too old to take up. But Sarah is just learning of her choices, all of which she relishes, lingers over. She asks to be woken early enough to consider every option of what to wear to school, and on the floor of the room she lays out possible outfits: shoes, tights, dresses, pants, shirts, socks. She does it for herself and for her little brother, and after they are dressed in the outfits they have picked and after they are gone, the rejected clothes remain.

The room I see is this: their sleeping selves are laid out, pajamas on his bed, nightgown on hers. Among table legs, train tracks, and Barbie gear his blue trousers and race car shirt pose solemnly. The shirt's long sleeve reaches toward that of Sarah's pink pullover, carefully tucked into the waist of a black skirt decorated all over with pink flowers. A second-choice skirt—she prefers the longer, purple one—it floats above the legs of red tights, legs splayed crazily as if in flight from this room, as if to remind us, and the attentive boy evoked by the posture of those empty dark blue trousers, that she is leaping forward into life. Soon she will not live in the bedroom next to ours. Soon she and Walker will have separate rooms, later separate homes and separate lives. This room will, perhaps, become the library we once imagined, the chaise re-covered in a studious leather or corduroy.

But for now the children are here, their room next to ours, his bed only nine steps from the one in which we sleep, hers fourteen.

## ALEX KOTLOWITZ

My brother, Dan, remembers our room as a great expanse of space, but in retrospect I think he simply confused space with time. "It just seems like most everything happened in there," he wrote me recently.

He's right. Our room did, indeed, seem cavernous. Big enough to house a makeshift basketball hoop made of wire hangers. Big enough to accommodate hamsters, gerbils, and a family of turtle doves. Big enough to be converted, long after my brother and I had left for college, into a combination guest room and study.

But it is what happened there that stays with me. There was no singular event, no explosive episode. Instead, the slow, evolutionary forging of a relationship. It is a construct that over time has withstood geographical distance, my brother's broken marriage, and the loss of our mother. The story of my bedroom is the story of filial fealty and friendship; it served, after all, as a place of comfort and security—and still does.

Three years into their marriage, my parents moved into a first-floor apartment of a high-rise on Manhattan's Upper West Side. Forty-two years later, my father still lives there. My parents were practical people, so there was little in the apartment that two rambunctious boys could damage. Oh, we had an elegant secretary in the dining room, which we learned, in later years, was designed by a renowned Italian furniture-maker and was among only two of its kind in the world. And my father had over time collected various prints and original paintings that I'm sure have appreciated in value. But beyond these collectibles, my parents, forever frugal, bought only what was comfortable and needed. The living-room couch went through at least two re-upholsterings; the metal kitchen chairs were from time to time outfitted with new cushions and, I believe, once received a new coat of paint. Those were our extravagances. It was as it should be.

The apartment was laid out in a fairly straight line, so it was impossible to pass through unnoticed. The dining room and kitchen were the first two rooms to greet visitors—the dining room to the left, the kitchen to the right. A living room big enough for a Steinway grand piano (which my mother inherited from her parents) served as the apartment's torso. There the family gathered, digesting crises and celebrations. There, our parents comforted us after the sudden death of our visiting grandmother and there, in later years, we gathered as a family to absorb and assimilate the news of my mother's recently diagnosed lung cancer. There, we also threw joyous bashes for both our parents on the occasion of their fiftieth birthdays—and once, in my parents' absence, my brother and I held a small, somewhat raucous party, empty beer bottles and vodka glasses left scattered around the room, picked up—wisely—before my parents' return. The two bedrooms, like afterthoughts, extended in opposite directions at the apartment's far end. Our parents' bedroom lay to the right. Ours was to the left.

The "boys' room." That's how the adults referred to it. It was a sliver of the house they rarely ventured into. Understandably. It smelled at various points in time of pubescent perspiration, of month-old wood shavings used to line a hamster cage, and of turds deposited by our doves, which, much to our parents' consternation, had free flight of the room. And to deter visitors—as if they needed deterring—we eventually installed a latch on the door.

I remember our room as a bright, airy place, but I know better. Our two windows overlooked a courtyard, and, because the apartment sat on the first floor, we received, if we were lucky, ten minutes of sunlight each morning. Moreover, rusting steel burglar bars deflected any early sun that might have crept between the high-rises east of us. We were so without daylight that our room could not sustain plants; it was so consistently dim that we could not tell the time of day. I keep meaning to ask my brother if this explains his eventual choice of profession: theatrical lighting designer. Did the lack of illumination stir his imagination?

The weather also passed us by. The room received no breezes; summers were so unbearably hot and stuffy that when we were very young my mother would administer wet washcloths to our foreheads as we lay awake at night unable to sleep. My brother remembers a hurricane hitting New York and his sitting by the window to view the violent winds. He saw nothing in that dark, bleak courtyard. Not even the pelting rain.

The windows, in retrospect, remind me of the barred openings afforded prisoners, except that ours, while certainly keeping us in, did not necessarily keep intruders out. At least on two occasions, small, wiry contortionists somewhat amazingly squeezed through what couldn't have been more than twelve-inch spaces left by the burglar bars. Once, my brother while occupied in the bathroom (he couldn't have been more than thirteen) heard a rustling noise coming from the far window. He flushed and went to look, peering upward at a ledge that ran the perimeter of the courtyard and was maybe a four-foot jump to our bedroom. He stared straight into the barrel of a silver revolver, whose owner, luckily, was a cop. Apparently, the police had been chasing a young man wanted for attempted murder, and one policeman's path led him through our bedroom window, through our apartment, and then into our building's lobby, where the man was apprehended. That window was also a thoroughfare for cats. A pregnant alleycat appeared in our bedroom one afternoon; our cat, named SheShe despite being a he, escaped numerous times through that aperture, once returning victorious after devouring a pigeon, his swollen stomach bouncing along the ground.

Indeed, my brother and I had little reason to look out our windows except for the couple of years when the School of American Ballet housed a group of young aspiring dancers in a brownstone across the courtyard. My brother and I would stand by the window and, with our elbows resting on the radiator and our heads peeping above the sill, yell our greetings to the frolicking girls. In the deepest voices we could muster, we would announce our ages, tacking on a couple of years in the hope that such maturity would lure these long-legged nymphs.

We slept in twin beds, which we regularly rearranged, probably because all other furniture in the house remained so static. We'd place them parallel to each other, at right angles, and on occasion side by side. They metamorphosed over time. They served as trampolines on which we'd perform death-defying flips. They served as battlefields on which we'd erect makeshift tents of sheets and blankets. They'd serve as fighting rings in which we'd wrestle and box, sometimes too earnestly. They were whatever we wanted them to be. They were the centripetal force in that room.

The other furniture was minimal. Along one wall stood a long, narrow black table that we shared as our desk. At various times, we had one or two chests of drawers, depending, I guess, on our wardrobe requirements. A bookshelf overflowed with books. On one wall, our parents had glued brown corkboard so that we could tack up pictures and other assorted memorabilia; we used it as a dart board, my brother once using our mom's good steak knives.

Had an archaeologist stumbled upon the room in later years, he would have had difficulty placing it in time. We had no pictures of our heroes: the Beatles or the Yankees. No pictures of Kennedy or King. The only hints would have been a bright orange poster depicting a peace sign and two chairs my parents purchased from the Polo Grounds when it closed. These hardback wooden chairs were painted a grass green, the orange seat

numbers still applied, and looked exotic in our beaten room—
but we used them little, because they were so damn uncomfort-
able. Our floor was covered with a dark brown shag carpet that,
at least for a while, hid the filth that only two boys can accumu-
late and shed. It was not an aesthetically pleasing room, but then
again we were a practical family.

I'm two years older than my brother and, quite frankly, remember little of our first few years together. Dan—or Danny, as
he was called until he insisted otherwise—contends that he can
recall my best friend and me plotting his murder as we sped a Li-
onel train around in endless circles. We were only four at the
time, and my brother says we wanted him out of the way. I'm
convinced that the story is apocryphal, but it has become part of
the family lore, a reminiscence to be told over and over again at
holiday gatherings. We shared this room for eleven years, until I
turned thirteen and in the throes of puberty and in my search for
privacy chose to move into a closet-sized room off the kitchen.
That is longer than I've lived with anyone else.

We shared much during that time. And fought even more. I
always had the bead on Danny, who until adolescence—when he
grew taller and sturdier—was shorter and rangier. We'd become
entangled in wrestling maneuvers so twisted and heated that inevitably matters would get out of hand; Danny would beg me to
stop, though that didn't prevent me from frequently bringing
him to tears. But that rivalry, intense as it was, never defined us
as brothers. We devoured books—and would share Hardy Boys
and Landmark biographies. We loved sports—and would play
one-on-one basketball using rolled-up socks as a ball. (In later
years, we played on our high school soccer team together.) We

competed—measuring our jumping ability by our handprints on the ceiling beams. We treasured animals—and bred turtle doves, three of which we named Nicky, Davinci, and Picasso, well ahead, I might add, of the Mutant Ninja Turtle craze. And like most boys we loved the mechanics and theater of war, spending hours creating elaborate battlefield scenes with tiny plastic soldiers—and then taking seconds to demolish the defenseless troops with pink Spaulding rubber balls and number-two pencils.

My brother and I implicitly understood the need to watch over each other. I left the bathroom light on to ease his fear of the dark. I walked him to school. I chastised him for hanging out with kids who I felt would only bring him trouble. (They did.) And Danny took care of me when, at the age of eleven, I underwent surgery for a hernia. The anesthetic administered had the effect of a narcotic. For three days, I hallucinated. I refused to leave my bed, repeatedly crying, "I want to go home." I ate little. I would periodically cry and gaze catatonically at the dirtied white walls of our room. My parents, as you might imagine, were quite frightened, especially since our doctor told them there was little he could do, that over the coming days the effects of the anesthetic would wear off. That seemed little consolation. I wouldn't acknowledge their presence. I wouldn't respond to their queries. Only my brother could make any kind of contact with me, and so my parents would send him into our room to sit at the end of my bed, where he'd ask questions and I'd babble. I don't remember what if anything he and I talked about, but I do know that his presence calmed and reassured me.

I don't know that I realized it then, but I hovered over my

brother, feeling simultaneously protected and protective. I knew where I was safe. I knew where I was needed. Many years later, when I was in my early thirties, our room appeared in my dreams, placed out of context in a massive, intricately detailed Victorian house, and while I could not pinpoint what I was running from in those nightly torments, the familiarity of the room accorded me shelter from what was clearly an emotional storm.

Dan now lives in Vermont, newly married. I live outside Chicago. We talk almost weekly and see each other regularly. We were best man at each of our weddings. I was the first to learn—over a beer in a grungy New York bar—of the breakup of his first marriage. And together we kneeled by the side of our mother's hospital bed as she lay dying, to listen to her last admonitions and advice. Weak from the chemotherapy and a bout with pneumonia, she managed a smile when Dan and I reassured her that we would watch after each other and our father; it comforted her, I'm sure, to know that, while we now lived half-a-country apart, we still shared a room.

The bedroom is now my father's study and a guest room. On our visits home, Dan and I sleep there, on a fold-out sofa. We both used it during our unemployed months after college. Over the years, we brought girlfriends there—and then our wives. And I lay there the night of our mother's death, consoled by the familiarity of the surroundings.

Little from our youth remains. The metamorphic beds are long gone—as are the desk, the doves, the peace poster, and the shag carpet. One of the white plaster walls has even been hammered away, exposing the aging redbrick. But stuffed in an antique wooden trunk are our childhood photos, diaries, and report cards, along with a baseball signed by the 1964 Yankees, a rusted hunting knife (given to me by a camp counselor), an assortment of 1960s-era campaign buttons, and a collection of turn-of-the-century silver dollars. In all these years, my brother and I have never removed these memorabilia. It's as if we want to keep a piece of ourselves in that room, to maintain some presence.

Recently, Dan, the lighting designer, wrote me, "I never really liked that room, and still don't. I think it's because there was never any light there." But there was.

## LYNDA BARRY

Keep Out. Keep OUT. THIS MEANS YOU. Keep! Out! But Mom always comes in with the bogus excuse of "Here are some clean socks and underwear, I'll put them in your drawer." As if I can't get my own socks and underwear from the laundry room, as if I need to get them at all, why can't I just keep them by the dryer but no, she just needs any excuse to come into my room and yell "This room looks like a tornado hit it!" as if she has ever seen anything hit by a tornado, and then she's coming back dragging the vacuum cleaner, as if she has the right to vacuum my room! I go, "MOM, NEVER VACUUM IN HERE!" I got too many important things of life on that floor. Stuff that dropped that I'll need later. And my tarantula who I swear to god hates my mom so much that the hairs fall off its abdomen which is what happens to tarantulas when they get

freaked and Mom is always freaking my tarantula with the vacuum. She said I could have a gerbil so I got a tarantula, tell me
what is the basic difference? I use the same fish tank that leaked
all over the dresser and wrecked it which I had to hear about for
five thousand years because that was her dresser when she was a
kid, SO WHY GIVE IT TO ME IF SHE DOESN'T WANT
ME TO WRECK IT! LIKE IT'S MY FAULT THE FISH
TANK LEAKED AND I DIDN'T NOTICE UNTIL ALL
THE WATER WAS OUT! WHAT ABOUT MY FISH, MOM,
HUH? WHAT ABOUT THEM DYING, MOM, HUH? So
that's why the dresser is all warped. It took a while for the water
to leak out. I just thought it was evaporating super fast. I thought
it was like a freak of the environment of my bedroom. CAN I
HELP IT IF IT WAS LEAKING DOWN THE SIDE OF THE
DRESSER I NEVER LOOK AT, MOM? And then you'd think
that if it was already wrecked she wouldn't care if I put my eye-
ball stickers on the mirror and the wood, right? A normal per-
son would normally think it's Already Wrecked So What's The
Dif? But she has a total attack and she has another total attack
that I put eyeball stickers on my bed, IT IS MY BED BUT SHE
HAS A TOTAL ATTACK, because it was her brother's bed or
her cousin's bed or someone of her family's bed WHO IS OB-
VIOUSLY MORE IMPORTANT THAN THE HAPPINESS
OF HER SON WHO JUST WANTS TO PUT HIS EYE-
BALL STICKERS WHERE HE WANTS EXCEPT HE
CAN'T BECAUSE HE LIVES IN A CONCENTRATION
CAMP. Same goes for tape and nail holes in the wall. I go,
"Mom, how am I supposed to put up my posters then?" and she
goes, "Oh, I'll buy you a bulletin board." THAT BULLETIN

BOARD RIGHT THERE WHICH I FILLED UP IN THREE
SECONDS WAS HER IDEA OF HOW I SHOULD PUT UP
MY POSTERS! I said forget it, man, this is boag, forget it. I'm
using tape and then she has another attack and makes me sign a
Family Contract that when I leave for college I will personally
paint my own room and sand down the tape marks or whatever
it is you do with tape marks, which I will have to figure out because as you have noticed there is hardly no wall showing. That
is my goal. Total posters. Including the ceiling. Oh, that's another
thing. You notice the green light bulbs, right? At first when I
bought them WITH MY OWN MONEY, MOM she totally
freaked because "Green light bulbs? Green light bulbs? The
neighbors will think you are growing drugs!" I go, Mom. What
kind of drugs do you grow with green light bulbs? I mean
SERIOUSLY! And she freaked and we had to have a family
meeting where my dad was even there which is totally weird because I think the total times my dad has even been in this room
is like around zero AND NOW HE GETS A VOTE ON MY
LIFE? Mom was freaking because she said it brought the value
of the house down because my bedroom used to be in the front
where the world could see it so that is how I scored this room
which used to be my sister's. It smelled like a girl for around a
month during which I couldn't have no one over but it was
worth it for the green light bulbs don't they make you feel
peaceful? Wait. Listen to this song. Isn't it the perfect combination? So I said can I get a gerbil, Mom? Because I wanted a tarantula but I knew she would totally freak if I said Can I Get A
Tarantula Mom EVEN THOUGH IT WAS MY OWN
MONEY and she goes, "Let me think about it." Which means I

have to do something like vacuum my room or change my sheets which I HATE because the laundry soap she uses smells like actual perfume, smell, smell here, doesn't it? Doesn't it smell exactly like perfume? Like I should go around smelling like that. But I go, OK Mom, I'll change the sheets, I'll vacuum if you'll let me have a gerbil and she goes, "I'll think about it." Which means I do something else for her like put new strings on the clothesline which I did, you can see them from this window, see there, pretty good job, right? So "OK," she says, "you can get the gerbil." And she says she'll take me down to Mitchell's Pets and I say No Mom That's OK I Want To Walk which if she was thinking about it she would have known right there because normally I don't want to walk anywhere. Normally I want to just listen to my station and lay in the peaceful green light and let my tarantula free its name is Dana for this girl Dana Speers at my school who I swear to god looks just like a tarantula but in a cool way. No one knows I named it Dana. They think I named it Boris. It would be embarrassing if people knew I named it after Dana Speers. My mom would get all happy. "Oh, a girl in my son's life!" So if she comes in, call it Boris. Actually I snuck the actual Dana Speers up here to meet Dana Speers the tarantula. Actually it is very easy to sneak people up here and to sneak out of here you can see how you can just go out that window and go down the roof to right there, then you just go onto the garage and down that tree. Cinchy. Dana Speers is a more interesting girl than normal. You wouldn't even think she's a girl from the way she is. She doesn't make no one nervous. I have sat right here and the actual Dana Speers has sat right where you are and we let the tarantula Dana Speers walk from my hand onto her hand then from her hand onto my hand, you know, that thing of letting a tarantula walk on you? And it was a trip because no hairs fell off the tarantula Dana Speers' abdomen when we did that which means that the tarantula wasn't nervous at all. Which shows you what I said about the actual Dana Speers. And she, the actual Dana, has these super-long eyelashes and eyebrows which some people think is freaky because it does look slightly monstery because there's hair all around her eyes, even right here in the corner part which I think looks insanely cool and you know that thing where if you get an eyelash from someone you can wish on it? And maybe even an eyebrow hair counts too, I don't know. I just know for sure that one eyelash fell off of the actual Dana Speers when she was last over but it would have been too weird of me to go for it while she was sitting there so I waited until after she left and I was looking for it and I am still looking for it because I got a really good wish I want to make and that's why I don't want mom to vacuum in here. That and also she might suck up my tarantula. Shhh! Here she comes! WHAT, MOM?! WHAT?! If she comes in Just Act Normal. Just sit there and act like you're normal. What?! OK! OK! I'M COMING!

## SUSAN POWER

The attic in Grandmother Power's home was a world of dust, cobweb curtains, bashful spiders, and family history. In 1973 I was eleven years old and unable to get a good night's sleep in that house. The few times I was alone on the second floor, I had the feeling I was being watched. *Don't be stupid,* I hissed to myself. But moments later I would run downstairs to join the others just the same. Now I think it was the attic that unnerved me. Perhaps I could feel it pressing down on the rest of the house, burdened with the family archives and memories, a museum gone to ruin. My mother, however, was intrigued by the idea of an attic. As a child she had lived in a log cabin, single story, where room was scarce, and no one ever accumulated enough objects to need storage.

"We'll check out the attic tomorrow," Mom told me, the night of our arrival.

The next day as my father settled his ailing mother in a nursing home just a few doors away from her own address, I followed
my mother up a narrow flight of stairs. Our hands brushed Oriental rugs that had been rolled so tightly they resembled columns
tipped on their sides—they lined the stair railing, wedged between the wooden rail and the wall. Mom and I stepped carefully across the floor, so blanketed by dust it felt as though we
were walking through powdery snow. We left tracks. We skirted
the stout trunks and leaning stacks of books to stand together
in a space free of clutter. We moved in a circle, a dance of confusion.

"Where should we begin," Mom said. It sounded more like
a decision than a question. So we set to poking through the contents of as many trunks and boxes as we could reach. With eager
hands we unearthed the only stories my mother didn't already
know.

"Your father's people sure are pack rats," Mom said, sounding both critical and delighted. I smiled because she had said *Your
father's people,* rather than *Your people*—a distinction of some im-
portance to me.

All my life my mother had told me that I was late being
born, I really took my time. I think I was just postponing the
confusion. Half Yanktonnai Dakota (Sioux) and half white, I tor-
tured myself with the obvious question: Whose side am I on
anyway? We lived in Chicago, halfway between my two grand-
mothers, midway between two worlds. Grandmother Kelly lived
on the Standing Rock Sioux Reservation in North Dakota, and
Grandmother Power lived in Albany, New York. Grandmother
Kelly was three years old when Sitting Bull was killed, and remembered seeing the wagon that brought his body to the

agency for burial. Grandmother Power graduated from Smith College and was later invited to join the Daughters of the American Revolution, though she declined. They were never brought together while they were alive, so they could meet only in me.

I felt distinctly Indian as my mother and I toiled in the attic, uncovering old secrets in letters, treasured mementos, faces in tintypes, names in Bibles, unread books. It was all so unfamiliar to us it was completely fascinating.

Among the pages my mother rescued from oblivion was a legal document that recorded the events surrounding the murder of my ancestor John M'Gilmore:

> *From the Plea Roll, in the reign of King Edward II, 1319: Robert Walsh was indicted at Waterford for killing John, son of Ivor M'Gilmore, and pledged that the said John was Irish, and that it was no felony to kill an Irishman.*
>
> *The King's attorney (John Fitz Robert le Poer) replied that M'Gilmore was an Ostman of Waterford, descended of Gerald M'Gilmore and that all his posterity and kinsmen were entitled to the law of Englishmen by the grant of Henry Fitz Empress, which he (the attorney) produced.*
>
> *And issue being joined, the jury found that on the first invasion of the English, Reginald the Dane, then ruler of Waterford, drew three great iron chains across the river to bar the passage of the King's fleet; but being conquered and taken by the English, he was for this tried and hanged by sentence of the King's court at Waterford with all his officers.*
>
> *They further found that King Henry the Second* [who reigned in 1154–1189] *banished all the then inhabitants of the town except Gerald M'Gilmore, who joined the English, and dwelt at that time in a tower over against the Church of the Friars.*

Mom chuckled to herself as she read the form. "People are crazy, aren't they? It was no felony to kill an Irishman, so they proved he was an Ostman. Well, we can certainly relate. There have been times when it wasn't a felony to kill an Indian, either."

My mother was mesmerized; she had released a legion of ghosts, a chain of lives. Our faces were smudged and our hair was powdered with dust; we began to perspire as the afternoon heat gathered in the room, although we couldn't be sure it was solely the work of the sun. Together my mother and I had invoked the spirits of my white ancestors—they heard their names spoken aloud for the first time in centuries. And who could blame them for thronging to that cluttered garret, jostling for elbow room and a comfortable perch? Their lonely breath filled the gabled space, leaving us less air to breathe, less room to maneuver. I can smile now at the irony: The Indians were prowling through the attic on a voyage of discovery, exhuming my dead Pilgrim fathers. Several of my ancestors had helped form the original colony in Massachusetts, one of them had signed the Declaration of Independence, a number of them had fought as patriots in the American Revolution, and one crafty collector had diligently acquired the autographs of the main players in the Civil War.

My mother was overwhelmed by the stories and the artifacts; she called out to me again and again: "Come take a look! *This* is your heritage too."

But in the end we were seduced by the memory of a young woman who had not gone to battle, been elected to public office, or founded an institution of higher learning, as had so many of the others. It was late in the day when we came across the plain wooden box that contained her life. Her name was

Josephine Parkhurst Gilmore, and she was born on October 8, 1841. She had been taken in as a child by the Parkhursts, who later adopted her when she was eighteen. She lived with her adoptive parents in Newton Centre, Massachusetts; her father was a minister, and she would marry Joseph Henry Gilmore (my great-great-grandfather), pastor of the Baptist Church of Fisherville (now Penacook), New Hampshire. The wooden box contained a packet of letters Josephine had written to her parents and a lock of her red-brown hair—the same dark shade as my own. Later we would find her wedding dress, crumpled inside a paper bag. I think it had been ivory silk trimmed with creamy white lace, but now it was the color of weak tea. We uncovered her tiny matching slippers—the satin covers and ribbon laces were still intact, and the soles unblemished. She must have worn them just the one time. The wedding shoes were so small and narrow my mother and I could barely manage to slip our hands inside them.

My mother studied the letters right there in the attic, beneath the faint light of a single bulb. She read me her favorite passages aloud, and I peered over her shoulder at the magnificent loops of Josephine's artful script.

"I wish I could write like that," I murmured.

Josephine's character seemed to us sunny and fine. She aspired to goodness, and confided to her mother at age seventeen: *Sometimes I can hardly believe that I am indeed a child of God. For when I consider all His benefits and how unmindful I am of them—it seems only just that He should cut me off.*

Josephine was deeply grateful to her parents for taking her in as a small child and raising her as their own. She told them: *I think*

*much of you and dear Father. You don't know how I feel toward you both*
*when I think of all of your kindness for me, my heart is big with grati-*
*tude often times when I can't speak. I often shudder when I think of*
*what I might have been if you had not had compassion for me. God will*
*reward you for it. I never can.*

Mom was tickled to learn that Josephine and her husband
honeymooned in Niagara Falls, like so many couples after them.
Josephine was nineteen years old and "Harry" twenty-seven
when they married, and their wedding trip was "glorious":

*In the short time I have been here I have got quite tanned up. I have*
*not as yet ascended any of the mountains about here. I don't think I*
*shall feel in any hurry about it—while there is so much to be seen at*
*the foot of them.*

*Harry, myself and a Mr. and Mrs. Thompson, a very pleasant*
*couple from Boston, went together to the Flume, Pool and Basin. We*
*had a charming excursion—such scenery and such climbing I never*
*saw. We went clear through the Flume as far as we could go and came*
*down outside of it. Then we took a charming walk through the woods,*
*part of the way logs serving us for bridges and after going down a very*
*steep pair of stairs we came to the Pool. I never enjoyed anything*
*more. Everything was so wild, so grand and so wonderful. Everything*
*said as plain as could be said: Behold the works of God.*

*There was a great old man at the Pool who paddled us about in*
*his boat. He is quite a philosopher in his way, and contends that the*
*earth is hollow and has a map to explain to people his theory. Some*
*wicked wag who knew the old man's eccentricities wrote a letter pur-*
*porting to be from Queen Victoria and sent it to him—the most*
*ridiculous letter it is that ever was seen, but he takes it for truth and*
*has facsimile copies of it for sale. I'll send you pretty soon. The origi-*
*nal he keeps in a glass case.*

I laughed at the mention of the elderly gentleman and his grand theory, but my mother said, "I wish we had that letter." He was clearly the sort of person she would enjoy meeting. Mom gasped as she read the paragraph a few lines farther down: *General Peirce and Hawthorne, the author of "Marble Faun," have been here. Harry seemed to be quite a pet with them. They wanted him to go fishing with them, so he went early this morning.*

"That's Nathaniel Hawthorne she's talking about!" Mom told me. "And he considered your great-great-grandfather a pet."

It was hard for me to imagine the stern, bewhiskered Joseph Henry Gilmore I had seen in photographs as anything but a solemn cleric, though there were indications of poetry in his blood, for he penned the lyrics to my favorite hymn, "He Leadeth Me."

During the next year my great-great-grandparents traveled extensively, and in her letters Josephine described trips to Brooklyn and Philadelphia. She was greatly impressed with the Liberty Bell. In all her travels Josephine's parents were never far from her thoughts. From Philadelphia she wrote: *Evening finds me in Mr. Watson's office to write just a little to my dear ones at home. I have been showing your daguerrotypes to the Watsons today and I shouldn't want to tell you the compliments which were paid you. I would like so much to see the dear originals tonight. I hope you are well and happy. I think of you many times a day.*

Finally, in 1862, Josephine was home in New Hampshire for a time. My mother's voice softened as she read a letter from this period: *I wish you could look out of my window for a few minutes and see the clouds come sailing up the north. Yesterday I went on a delight-*

*ful jaunt to see some cattails—on the way I picked and had picked for me over fifty Indian pipe flowers which are very rare. Then I picked a lot of myrtle, wild myrtle; it is like ours only more graceful, and with these I trimmed my hair and Aunt Nancy's. I have my hair trimmed with one thing and another, every night. I wish you might have seen the leaves I had the other night—maple they were—some of them were a deep green with red spots and stripes in them, others pure red, etc., beautifully turned by the frost. There are quantities of beautiful things here to dress my hair with—if one will look for them.*

The attic was growing dark and I was suddenly weary of my great-great-grandmother's reasonable voice. *Was she never persnickety?* I wondered. *Was she never cross?*

"Listen to this," Mom said, laughing. With great relief I heard the following censure: *Sallie Smith and I hardly speak to each other now. She snubbed me in the most pointed manner when I first came, until she found I was getting more attention paid me than she was, but then it was too late and I had had enough of her ways, and I just avoid her. I treat her politely, but no more. She is generally disliked and no wonder; her "stuckupishness" don't go down with anyone. She is a great hypocrite and a mischief maker.*

Josephine Parkhurst Gilmore wasn't perfect after all. This was an ancestor I could accept as family.

Shortly before leaving my grandmother's attic Mom reached the last letters at the bottom of the box. They had been written in 1863. We quickly learned that Josephine was pregnant and her baby due at the end of September. In August she caught a cold she couldn't shake, and the girl begged her mother to come for a visit: *In addition to my cold I have the old complaint that summer brings. Of course I am weak, very. I try to keep up good courage and I haven't fairly broken down yet, but it is hard work. I have sent a telegram to father this morning and Lucy is still in Concord waiting for an answer to it. The Browns are all at home now. So you may feel safe about me I shall have good care.*

*I wish you could be with me my last month. I think I need you as much then as at the time, and perhaps more. I don't seem to have any heart to take hold and get things ready. I may feel differently when I get better though. It would be so nice to have you here to arrange with me.*

Two days later she mailed another entreaty:

*I don't want to alarm you but I feel as if I must have you with me. I wanted to send for you but felt as if it would be perhaps foolish to do so, but Mrs. John Brown thinks I ought to. She has been with me all the afternoon rubbing and bathing me and wants me to send for the doctor but I had rather not, but I will send for you. Harry can't get back before the last of next week and with worrying about him and feeling really sick from this heavy cold, I don't feel safe to be alone. I can't sleep nights and really I am miserable and at this time I think I am not safe in being alone. Now won't you please come up and stay this week with me? I will pay your expenses very willingly. Won't you come up on the early train Tuesday?*

*At any rate I shall look forward to your being with me and that will help me to feel a little better. Father will be willing I know under the circumstances to let you come. I am not in the habit of complaining, you know, and I would not send for you now if I could get along without you. I have taken to my bed this afternoon—I have tried to sit up until I have lost all backbone. I am so sorry this cold should come just now. Now don't disappoint your daughter.*

"Why doesn't she go?!" I wailed, caught up in the drama. "It wasn't that far, was it?"

"No," Mom answered. "Just Boston to New Hampshire, though it took a lot longer to get around in those days." Perhaps she noticed my distress, for she patted my hand. "I would be there in a second."

Mary Parkhurst did make the journey, it turned out, though she stayed for only a few days. In her final letter Josephine again urged her mother to visit:

*September 6, 1863*

*My dear mother,*

*I wish you could be with me today. I am not feeling well at all and as Aunt Maria has not yet returned, I am a bit lonely while Harry is at church. I have managed to take a little more cold and I am so stiff and sore that I can hardly get up or down. I am getting very clumsy anyway—It seems as if I could hardly wait three weeks longer. I want you to be on hand early, Mother.*

*My room isn't put in order yet for the reason the stove man has been away and so I couldn't have the stove set. I thought it best to make only one job of it.*

*Harry was in Boston last week. He was obliged to go to his cousin Fred's funeral. He went down in the early train Friday and back in the early train Saturday. He had no time to go to see father. What do you think he brought me home? A basket of delicious fruit, pears, plums and grapes. They were luscious.*

*It seemed like old times at Newton. When I used to be ill, don't you know how very thoughtful he always was. If our lives are only spared what a happy family ours will be after the little one comes. I do pray that God may grant to us a dear little child and good health.*

*Mrs. John Brown has been in today to see me. She seems to take a great interest in me. I think a good deal of her judgement—she has had experience you know.*

*I will write you again next week, but am too tired to prolong this epistle. Come up as soon as you can. With a great deal of love to father and yourself.*

*I am, your daughter,*
*Josie Gilmore*

*There are two or three plants I want you to buy for me to bring up with you; a mahunia, a white camilia what they call candidissima and a plant called colisium ivy. Father can buy these in Boston you know, and you can bring them up with you, can't you? They will of course all be small plants. Goodbye again. Love to the Smiths when you see them.*

On September 9, Josephine gave birth to Joseph Henry Gilmore, Jr., and on September 11, she died.

My mother and I huddled together in the attic, two more shadows lost in the disorder. Mom returned the letters and the lock of hair to the heavy box. We folded the brittle wedding dress as gently as we could, smoothing a century of wrinkles.

"Her little boy must have kept these things so he could feel close to the mother he never knew," Mom said. "He was your Daddy's grandfather, and Daddy worshiped him. He was gentle and mischievous, and loved your father."

When Mom and I left the hushed attic it was as if we had returned to life, the way I have felt on emerging from church into afternoon light. We rescued the family papers and the stories they contained, and we still tell them to one another, though my mother tells them best. We know what happened to "Harry" and his son, and for us it is like looking into the future. Two years after Josephine died, Joseph Henry Gilmore married Miss Lucy

Brown, who had been a dear friend of Josephine's, and one of her nurses at the end. She was a good mother to Josephine's child and gave him five siblings.

My grandmother died three months after Mom and I explored her attic, and the house was sold. It has been twenty-two years since that last visit.

My mother is proud of her Dakota forebears and the Sioux Nation she comes from, but she has encouraged me to find both sides of myself, and so, undiminished, I have become whole.

"You gave me a great gift," I should tell my mother the next time I telephone. But it is hard for me to say these things.

My mother and I visited Josephine Parkhurst Gilmore's grave at the start of my sophomore year in college. I remember I was bored and a little irritated as we wandered through the old section of the Newton Cemetery. I was anxious to meet a new roommate and wanted the school year to begin; I couldn't be bothered with ancestral spirits who were lonesome for company.

"She is here somewhere," my mother told me. "Concentrate."

I don't know why we didn't go through proper channels, why we didn't visit an office and ask for a map of the burial plots—there must have been records. But we conducted this search on our own, without benefit of bureaucracy, and I felt a little like a skeptic handling a dousing stick. I squinted at the worn gravestones, following a path my mother suggested, and just minutes after we stepped from the car I found Josephine settled between her parents.

"Over here," I called to my mother a little gruffly. It had all

worked out just as she'd promised. I had found my relative so easily because she longed to be discovered and remembered. But I
couldn't stand for my mother to be right.

"It's just a coincidence," I mumbled.

"Just think, you've found her," Mom whispered. "Josephine
Parkhurst Gilmore, this is your great-great-granddaughter." My
mother made the introductions and I probably squirmed a little,
peeked over my shoulder to be certain we were alone, unob-
served. I was poor company.

Mom cried a little. "It's the Irish in me," she teased, and she
brushed a hand across the face of Josephine's marker. "Let's find
a stone to remind us of this place." We uncovered a flat triangu-
lar rock and Mom wrapped it in Kleenex tissue.

I know my mother must have told Josephine that I was a
sophomore at Harvard, because it wouldn't be rude to brag to
another relative. Surely she mentioned we were Indian, Dakotas,
and wondered what Josephine would make of that. She could
have lectured the girl, telling her that on September 3, 1863—
just three days before Josephine Parkhurst Gilmore penned her
last letter—the peaceful village of my great-great-grandfather
Chief Two Bear had been attacked by Generals Sibley and Sully,
and our Yanktonnai band nearly wiped out.

My mother has described the scene so vividly I sometimes
think she must have been there, urging the dogs to run swiftly
from the slaughter, dragging babies strapped to miniature travois
behind them. Her nostrils quiver when she tells me that the soldiers burned the camp and the winter stores of food, and I know
she can smell the fragrance of that wasted buffalo meat and taste
the melting tallow.

But all my mother said to Josephine was "I hope your mother was there at the end. I know you weren't alone, but your husband or a friend wouldn't be the same comfort, would they? There are times when only a mother will do."

*Yes,* I can tell her now, *there are times.* I can agree because I am older. I finished college and then law school and then a writing program. I wrote a book. After all this education I have finally learned that I will never know as much as my mother. I stand happily in her shadow, no longer annoyed by her faith and imagination. I ask her to repeat the stories. I strain to hear her voice.

And the next time my mother visits me in Cambridge, Massachusetts, I will suggest we return to the Newton Cemetery. We will wander through the old section, patiently searching for the young lady we visited once before. This time I will be more polite, ready with presents I offer my great-great-grandmother, who is now twelve years my junior.

"Mom, look," I will whisper as I unwrap the papers. The wild myrtle is a brilliant blue—it should look fine twisted in the intricate crown of Josephine's brown hair; the white camellias are soft, snowy, and will cover her slight figure like a blanket of lace.

## JAMES FINN GARNER

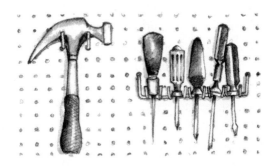

It wasn't until I owned my own house—and spent countless hours ripping down plaster, installing conduit, painting trim, and generally correcting the insults and injuries inflicted on the building by its previous owners—that I began to realize what keen observers of the human condition the Three Stooges were. The way we hurt those we are most trying to help, the chaos and destruction that lurk beneath the surface of our interactions, the yearning for the grail in our fruitless attempts at inventing spotted paint—anything profound I might have had to say about the difficulties of striving to maintain a livable space for myself and my young family had already been expressed far more eloquently by a trio of short and extremely homely ex-vaudevillians.

Nevertheless, since, as Nietzsche said, "That which does not

kill us gives us something to brag about at barbecues," I soon became pretty flip with home improvement advice for anyone unlucky enough to be around. It seemed only equitable that those
wishing to be initiated into the ranks of the home owner should
have to make as many mistakes and sift through as much misin-
formation as I did. Adding the modifiers "flange," "toggle," or
"grommet" to any recognizable hardware word would quickly
send inexperienced or passingly knowledgeable fixer-uppers
into retreat. Combining all three—thus creating the "flange toggle grommet"—was the trump, to be used only against those
climbers who had purchased much bigger houses than mine.

A few months after our own purchase, my older brother
Patrick and his wife bought their first home, a big lovely house
of the Arts and Crafts school. Since their home still reflected a
recognizable style, any work they had to do would need more
care; our house was of old yet indeterminable style, so all we
needed to do to receive compliments was keep the cracks in the
plaster patched and refrain from painting in Day-Glo colors.
With thirty years of apartment living between us, Pat and I both
faced the ominous revelation that we and we alone were responsible for fixing our own plumbing, and that certain now-in-
dispensable tools were just too big to fit in the kitchen drawer.
After much commiseration, my brother and I fixed on a solution
independently, yet almost simultaneously: our problems would
be over if we could only build a big workbench like our father's.

The irony of this panacea would be lost to everyone but my
family and our old neighbors. My father was as adept at household repairs as a seagull at snooker. For Pat and me to invoke his
spirit by building a workbench would be like taking singing

lessons to emulate William Shatner. But we were each bound and determined to erect an elaborate workbench—complete with a vice, a pegboard wall, and little screwdriver wells—to pattern ourselves after our father, who, left on his own, would have had a devil of a time assembling a functional breadboard.

While our father was not in any way good or ambitious in the area of home improvement, he did enjoy the use of the workroom in our house as his *sanctum sanctorum*. Almost every man I've ever met has expressed the need and desire for a similar locale in his life, a place where he can work or not work at his own pace, somewhere to pursue doomed experiments and wrong ideas, someplace where his failures would not be on public display—indeed, where such efforts would not be failures at all. So utterly convinced of his ineptitude around the house, my father really didn't spend an inordinate amount of time down in the workroom. That might have led to home repair ambitions, which in turn would have led to projects, which probably would have led to some failures, which I don't think he would have allowed himself to have. He did, however, have his space.

Even with its lack of use, my memories of the workroom are as strong or stronger than for any other room in our home. A trip to the workroom was a mainly sensory experience; the sounds, the smells, and even the light seem so specific to that time and place. The activities I remember most in the room were my father soaking his paintbrushes in turpentine-filled orange-juice containers within arm's length of our old furnace, and cleaning his nails with an ivory-handled steak knife of unknown origin. And always, always with a Winston in his mouth. It would be nice if I could describe the hours of worldly wisdom that passed

from father to son in patient exchanges and Platonic dialogue—
what our more dithery era has christened bonding. It would
have been nice, had it ever happened. My father was almost
pathologically tight-lipped, and my brothers and I had to absorb
what lessons we could from example and, in the home repair
realm, from non-example.

My family lived in a simple brick postwar Georgian, boasting
nothing elaborate or eccentric in its layout. The workroom was
merely the corner of the basement taken up partially by the
water heater and the massive old furnace, set apart by an L-
shaped wall of then-ubiquitous knotty pine paneling, heavily
lacquered to a spotty orange-chestnut hue. The room was thus
consigned to the corner both physically and symbolically. Had
we lived in an older house—well, that's moot. There's no chance
we ever would have lived in an older house. Too many things
could go wrong that would need fixing.

The door to the workroom was one of those swinging sa-
loon-type doors, misaligned just perfectly so that its every use
created a three-and-a-half-beat signature sound—*bada . . . bada
. . . bada . . . ba*—that could be heard throughout the house. If
you were dainty with this door, you would invariably catch your
fingers in it, so the best course of action (especially for young,
role-playing boys) was to burst through it like Jack Palance with
a bug up his chaps. The only light fixture in the room also made
a unique and definitive sound. A bulb with a metal shade suspended from the ceiling, the light had a chain pull that would recoil when yanked and elicit a skittery, sustained Oriental *clang*

from the metal shade, announcing your presence in the room like a gong.

Although prone to strange and sometimes silly outbursts that were apropos of nothing ("Ya-ha, San Antone!" was not uncommon), my father was a taciturn man. One of the few aphorisms I can remember from him was "When you're talking, you ain't thinking," a not-so-subtle hint that conversation was an annoyance unless and until someone had something important to say. He could be intense at times, such as when he was problem-solving, but he worked hard at keeping a placid facade even when something was eating him up inside. His job, which he kept almost entirely apart from his home life except for the toll it took on his nerves and heart, was to borrow money on the commercial paper market, where a brief lapse in attention on competing interest rates can cost thousands. (I didn't understand this until I met the man who succeeded my father in his position. This man, who was in his thirties, told me he wouldn't be able to do the job more than four years before burning out; my father did it for sixteen.) This mental intensity did not serve Dad well in the role of Mr. Fix-it. Tiny mistakes grew and nagged at his sense of order and his need for tranquillity. If something couldn't be done perfectly, it wasn't worth doing at all.

If you side with the genetic proponents of the Nature vs. Nurture debate, you might find my father blameless in his workshop ineptitude, a victim of duff-handed determinism. According to my mother, my paternal grandfather was, if anything, worse around a tool than my father. In the late 1940s, Grandpa invested in the type of freestanding power tools that make most men salivate: a huge table saw, a jigsaw, and a lathe, each immensely heavy, in the dimpled olive green and chrome deco style of the Sears Craftsman variety. With all these impressive embodiments of American industrial might at his command, the only item Grandpa ever produced was the core of a toilet paper holder. My eldest brother, Tom, has since sold these behemoths to a tool collector, the type of man who loves to spend hours cleaning, fixing, and oiling old machines that either have been used within microns of their useful life or stand as mute testimony to unfulfilled mechanical ambition. What weird individuals these types must be.

Although I never knew him, in an abstract way Grandpa's lack of skill sometimes surprises me more than my father's. Often people from impoverished backgrounds are so frugal that throwing money away at a repairman is considered almost as bad as discarding a ham bone without first making soup. In 1910, with the proverbial dime in his pocket, my father's father arrived in Montreal with his sister and brother, hard and undersized children of a deceased greengrocer from Liverpool. Perhaps, along with his accent and any false nostalgia for Old Blighty, he chose to discard any reminders of his cruel and dirt-poor background, including working with his hands.

The tool with which my father was most proficient (if I might be so generous as to use the word) was the hammer. This might reflect his pronounced tunnel vision and his ability to cut right to the main thrust of any problem. The hammer is a quintessential and versatile tool. Maybe any job that needed an implement more complicated was best left to specialists. This attitude persisted despite the well-intentioned advice of neighbors. Shortly after we moved into our house, our neighbor Mr.

Weier visited and offered in all sincerity the sage advice, "You know, there are other tools besides the hammer." If there were, my father wasn't interested.

When I was very young, Dad put together a few projects for my brothers, which consisted mainly of large sheets of uncut plywood. Nail some two-by-fours around the perimeter of a piece of plywood, add a bit of green and brown paint, and the result was a landscape for a train set. Attach three tall sheets of plywood together with hinges like a triptych, cut out a medium-sized hole in the middle sheet, add a small curtain—ta-da, a puppet theater! (As the youngest, I guess I was expected to inherit these things, because I don't remember any large-scale project intended for me. Then again, I can count on the fingers of one hand the large-scale projects ever attempted during my youth.) At some point, my father erected three stalls at the foot of the basement stairs for our coats, along with cubby holes for our Frisbees and baseball mitts; we greeted this accomplishment with loud huzzahs. This miraculous construction was on a par with the erection of a tree fort with swimming pool.

During my grade school years, my father did something that allowed him to expand his manual non-dexterity in new and untested areas: he invested in a boat, first an old, blunt-nosed Matthews cabin cruiser with much too much wood to varnish, and later a slightly bigger Egg Harbor. When these two boats had been built, fiberglass was still an exotic element. Their wooden hulls and teak decks were in need of constant work, a race against their inevitable mortality that my father could never win. At this time the smells that I will always associate with our workroom were introduced—varnish, hull paint, Mr. Thinzit, and Cuprinol.

And cigarettes, always cigarettes. These ineradicable odors permeated and formed an olfactory link between the workroom, the boat, and my father's no-frills, putty-beige Ford Maverick. And also his horrifically paint-splattered Top-Siders, which my mother could never persuade him to toss out.

I don't know whether my father bought the boats to get away from the worries of work or the worries of the house or neither. He got his main relaxation from the nautical lifestyle on Friday nights, when he would sit on the back deck with a Stroh's in his hand, staring upriver at the seven smokestacks of the Edison plant, and think grand thoughts. (At least, I thought they were grand—they were certainly elaborate and beyond my comprehension at the time. Asking an open-ended question at times like these would trigger an inundation of fact and opinion that would make me wish I'd taken his example and figured it out for myself.)

By Saturday, the aggravations of the physical world would reappear. General maintenance, such as scrubbing the teak deck, was ongoing. The big engines would regularly break down during the course of the summer, giving Dad another lesson in humility in the face of mechanical demands. Leaning into the big hatches in the deck, he would sweat and strain with the monstrous creations, using words he would never use in any other situation. His hammer had by this time been replaced by a monkey wrench. The increased variety of striking surfaces the wrench offered might have been seen as an improvement on the hammer, but the banging was as ineffectual as ever. Invariably a neighboring boat owner would come by, or a mechanic from the marina across the river would motor over, and with a few deft moves solve the insoluble and fix the unfixable. Dad would stand by, eager to learn and almost completely untrainable. After a dozen years of this, the transom of the boat was almost completely gone from dry rot, and Dad decided it was time to be rid of such "relaxation." His own health was also beginning to break down at this time.

When I was a teenager, the workroom saw even less use than it had in previous years. Still, it was the only place to finish certain messy projects with paint and putty. Whenever I was down there, in memory it seems like I could always find a Tigers game on the radio. The radio of choice in the workroom was one of those round, "mod" cheapos from Panasonic, with the dimensions of a ruby grapefruit and nearly the sound quality. (Our basement was a radio graveyard—at least half a dozen were scattered around, in various states of workability, all sounding atrocious.) Next to the white round radio on the workbench sat another essential spherical accoutrement, my father's eight-ball ashtray—nine or ten inches tall, rusty, malignant, uncaring, and immovable.

In my freshman year of high school, the workroom was witness to the most elaborate science fair experiment anyone in my family had ever attempted. I hated science fairs vehemently, both bored and intimidated by the subject matter and its challenge to my academic record. However, I managed to find an experiment in a library book that actually intrigued me. Over the strenuous objections of my mother, I bought six newly weaned white mice, paired them off in separate small glass habitats, and fed them diets of varying quality to see how it would affect their growth as they matured. Not surprisingly, the two that were fed nothing but sugar and bacon grease were small, jumpy, and inclined to bite your fingers when touched (not unlike myself in those years, I now realize). I won a ribbon in the city-wide competition that year, and sold my exhibit to a classmate's sister for her own use later. The valiant mice, their lives already dedicated to science and the education of young minds, became lunch for the boa constrictor in a local third-grade classroom. The next year, to protest mandatory participation in science fairs, I prepared an elaborate display describing in detail the scientific principles of embalming and related funerary practices. It didn't win a ribbon.

My hometown owes its current size and prosperity to that workshop putterer par excellence, Henry Ford, whose very name strikes fear and awe into the hearts of the world's mechanically disinclined. What these people may not realize is, when Ford built his first workable horseless carriage, he failed to take into account the width of his garage door. Undaunted, he took a hammer and knocked away the bricks on either side of the portal so he could drive out. Shades of Larry, Moe, and Curly.

One of Ford's many side projects was assembling an enclave of historic buildings, in which the preeminent tinkerers and mechanical whiz kids of American industrial history had clocked some hours. Over time it became a tourist destination called Greenfield Village. My mother and my brother Patrick worked there seasonally, and one year my mother convinced the head of the crafts department that I was good with my hands, her sole evidence being a precut pine bookshelf that I had pieced together and secured with a dozen finishing nails. So I was hired for the summer, and one cold rainy day in May I was assigned to work in a one-room cooper shop built in 1795. In addition to two hundred years of grime and a fireplace in which a half-dozen people could stand comfortably, it boasted three rough but phenomenally well used workbenches.

I was cursorily educated in the art of barrel-making (or at least the remedial coopering done by apprentices) by a patient and affable man in his seventies who could demonstrate many of the other crafts around, such as tinsmithing and leatherwork, with admirable skill. While he had the gait and demeanor of someone who'd been a handyman all his life, I found out later he had been involved in groundbreaking statistical work that was used in the creation of the UNIVAC. Carving water buckets and butter churns out of warped, grainy hemlock planks entirely by hand was not the easiest thing I had ever done. On the other hand, it was not something that the average tourist knew anything about. So with a little flair and misdirection, I could easily take attention away from my slip-ups with the draw knives (except of course when I drew blood). My numerous mistakes didn't cause anyone any grief, and were usually burnt as tinder in some other exhibit. My successes were used to decorate my work area, and were occasionally taken away for sale. The tourists rarely pointed out what I was doing wrong—they could scarcely understand what I was doing anyway, or why—and my bosses just wanted me to stay chatty and informed. Thus, flying in the face of my genetic inheritance, I finally taught myself to enjoy puttering around a workbench, experimenting and exploring for the fun of it. Suddenly my manual mistakes no longer seemed life-threatening or divinely predetermined. During the winter holidays, I was hired back, to make wooden toys and carve baby rattles on a foot-powered lathe once owned by Thomas Edison.

Many times I would drive after work, covered in sawdust and linseed oil, to pick up my father at the world headquarters of the company Ford had founded so many decades earlier. It somehow felt very grown-up to do this, a "two men on their way home after a hard day's work in the salt mines" kind of feeling. It's not like we ever talked about anything profound. I'd complain about the ridiculous questions the tourists would ask ("For years I've heard of 'the old oaken bucket'—what did they make those out of, anyway?"). Dad would just mock my exasperation and say, "You tell 'em, Jimbo, you tell 'em!" I felt like an adult because the gap between what we needed to know about each other's passions and our ability to communicate was widening. I knew it would continue to grow before it had any hope of narrowing.

Dad had already had at least one heart attack by this point, and was supposed to be easing up on his workload. He was still putting in eight-hour days, though, and more than likely was still feeling too much stress. After his second heart attack, he more or less was confined to home. At this time of life, many men take to their workrooms and begin to create furniture, fix old engines, or rehab their homes or garages. Of course, this was not an option in our home. With his time now his own, Dad channeled his energies in an entirely unexpected direction.

For years, the only attention my father had given to plant life was a few treatments of Milorganite on the lawn in the spring. After his heart had effectively retired him, he began to work earnestly to turn our small backyard into an elaborate, even overstocked garden. At the same time, his workbench was retired too, and transformed into a sort of makeshift greenhouse. Rows and rows of flower seedlings incubated there in the winter and spring under the grow lights, cozy next to the furnace in their little cups filled with peat. The smells of paint and solvent in the workroom began to fade, but never disappeared.

Dad poured himself into that garden and was, I think, very gratified with how well it did in such a short time. Phlox, impatiens, lilies, and petunias now spilled forth from among the stalwart, low-maintenance evergreens, and by summer's end the backyard was a carnival of color. A few plantings might have failed to take, but these were nothing compared with the teeming beauty he was now adept at bringing forth.

"Why are you bothering to grow these things?" I would tease him. "What good are they? You can't eat any of them."

"Add a little beauty to the world, Jimbo," he would intone in his characteristic way, as if calling to me from across a chasm, "add a little beauty to the world."

Dad used to wear a wide straw hat when he worked in the garden, to protect his Anglo-Irish skin from the sun. Whenever he wore it, I called him "Brother Orchid," after an old gangster movie in which Edward G. Robinson went on the lam and hid in a monastery, where he learned to till the most glorious gardens. Although he never said so, I think Dad liked it when I called him this—he was the kind of guy who liked to use a lot of nicknames.

My father got to enjoy his new garden for only a couple of summers before his heart rebelled one last and irrevocable time.

Among so many other things he has since missed, he never got to visit the many ramshackle apartments I've lived in, and was never able to offer advice to me or my brothers when we bought our first houses. It's probably only a coincidence, but my brothers and I all have fathers-in-law who are incredibly adept around a workroom. I often wonder how my dad would get along with my wife's father, Dave, an ebullient and inquisitive man who is as given to superlatives as my father was to silence. I'm next to positive that a great deal of goodwill would ignite in the spark between these two opposites, but I know that the Saturday morning work detail (which is now compulsory around our house, ever since I married into good Calvinist stock) would be a trial. For one thing, Dave's workbench is too well organized and complete, and for another thing, it gets used.

It is now a standing family joke that my brothers and I inherited, along with his high forehead, double chin, and intractable stubbornness, my father's ten thumbs. This generalization persists despite growing evidence to the contrary. Tom has done a good job around his houses, although he seems predisposed to new construction, and Pat has practically gutted the second and third floors of his house (of course, putting it back together is another proposition entirely). I myself have torn apart about three quarters of our house in the past two years, although the help of others—including my wife's cousin, who is currently building his own house without the aid of blueprints—has been indispensable. Our current house has a small workroom—basically just the area under our back porch, walled off, uninsulated and unfinished. Only a very imaginative real estate agent would describe it as a workroom. I have yet to build the big workbench I've dreamed of.

My wife's father would object to the generalizations about my ineptitude as a handyman. He is, however, the soul of charity. When my in-laws visit on the weekends, Dave always brings along work clothes, and I prepare for my next tutorial. He and I agree that you have to be willing to make some mistakes if you want to become a good handyman. And believe me, I can make mistakes as quickly as anybody, then ponder them intensely while I wait for the proper time (and assistance) to solve them. But what the hey, it's my house. If home means anything, it's a place where you're allowed to make mistakes. I think this is the lesson that always eluded my father.

The legacies my brothers and I received are so numerous and pervasive that my inadequacies in the workroom have never bothered me. Of course, these legacies become more apparent with age, as does my acceptance of them. My niece Hannah Rose now sleeps in the crib that my father assembled for his sons. It unmistakably belongs to our family. My mother only has to point to the side of the crib and explain, "That's when your dad threw the little felt washers across the room and just tried to force the pieces to fit."

There in the blond wood, you can clearly see the crescent marks left by the impatient hammer of my father.

# GISH JEN

## 1. THAT WHICH WAS OUR GARAGE

That which was our garage is now our luau room. We've taken two walls out of it. We've put in brick arches of the pizza oven type, only larger. There is also a bluestone floor; and the problem ivy that used to grow up our neighbor's wall, under our rafters, and into the garage is no longer a problem. Now it is a feature. An ivy cascade! It could be right out of Martha Stewart—a perfect backdrop for a buffet table laden with pineapple boats and cornball drinks. In short, our garage has become the kind of space in which resorts used to set up their theme cookouts, and when I think of mortality, and our short moment on earth, and what it means to seize the day, I realize that I will not die truly happy until we have had a pig roast there, with coconut bowling out on the lawn.

We are awaiting an appropriate occasion. A wedding? A baby

shower? It has only been six months since the luau room came into our lives, but we are impatient. Luckily, we have other activities to pursue in the luau room. Crafts, for instance. (My husband, Dave, and I have a preschooler, Luke.) We want to do papier-mâché volcanoes, egg carton igloos. We want to picnic out there in the warm weather, and for the cold weather we have bought (for half price) a Lillian Vernon inflatable ice-skating rink; add schmaltzy music and we can have winter wonderland parties. The luau room is also a good space for other parties: for Luke's third birthday we had a Russian puppeteer perform under the ivy cascade, and while this was not the same as having a luau, it was nonetheless great fun. (We had box juice instead of tacki-tacki drinks, and a cake with an excavator on it.)

Is the luau room actually a gazebo? It depends, I suppose, on whether a gazebo can have a storage shed across the back and be partly made of cinderblock. An architect friend says it's a folly, and that seems closer to the truth, except that the essential nature of follies has always seemed to me ornamental. This seems to be a folly crossed with a multipurpose room—multipurpose room being the name of a certain (multipurpose) room in the elementary school I transferred into in fifth grade. (This was Greenacres Elementary, in Scarsdale, New York.) How up-to-date that name seemed then!—and how much it epitomized the difference between my ex-school and my new school. My ex-school was St. Eugene's in Yonkers, New York—a Catholic school in a working-class neighborhood where a small class had forty kids in it, and some classes had sixty. Every room was a classroom except the bathroom. We played out in the parking lot, and for a jungle gym we had the steps leading up to an all-weather Virgin Mary. I seem to remember some metal handrails, too, and of course there was the chain-link fence. Our new school, on the other hand, had swings! A library! Overhead projectors! And of all things, a multipurpose room. From the school's point of view, this was probably an overbooked space expected to accommodate way too many needs. But from my point of view, it was an extra room; and this was an unimaginable thing. An extra room! In a school!

I am still thinking about it, thirty years later. Thirty years later, the proud owner of a garage turned luau room, I am still thinking about extra rooms, and undesignated space. What does the presence of such space say to us? In some places, it says that there may be important human activities that do not easily fit into conventionally planned space; that the community can afford unnecessary activities; and that these activities are even to be encouraged. In other places, it says simply that there is surplus space, who knows why; in others still, that this place does not matter to society, that nobody cares enough to claim it.

Do these distinctions matter, necessarily, to the imagination? In my new fifth-grade world, there was this amazing multipurpose room, with sliders and partitions—a consciously flexible space, a legitimate space. But in my old world, we had, behind our old house, just beyond the brave row of knee-high hemlocks that formed our someday-to-be-a-hedge, a large stretch of woods. There were gargantuan rocks there, with deep holes that filled with water, and one of my earliest memories is of reaching into one of those holes and discovering that the water had mysteriously turned to ice. I can still remember the shape of the hole, how cylindrical it was; and that all around me was a brilliant fall day, nowhere near winter yet. I remember that there were two other holes, both of which merely held cold water. But in that one hole there was ice; and I remember that I poked at that ice and felt it resist me, as solid a thing as the rock around it. I remember that a patch of light fell on the hole and on the surrounding rock, and that I found that patch inexplicably satisfying. I remember that on the way home there was a big daytime moon.

Did I learn anything from that? About ice? About the rock? About the moon? As usual, I learned nothing. I am a child of immigrants, which is to say a child of busy parents. There was no one to explain things to me; no one got out the encyclopedia and looked up this or that. I am a person who learned things eventually—who, not knowing any better, quite enjoyed learning nothing in particular. About ice; about the hand- and footholds on Elephant Rock; about where mushrooms sprang up, and how it felt to sit on a rotted log. I talked to myself a lot out in the woods, and there is no question in my mind that that was the beginning of becoming a writer for me; that I began, not by having a role model, or by being encouraged to read and write, or by being given a typewriter, but by wandering around, unsupervised, to no purpose.

There was danger in the woods, of course—not real danger as we know it today, but there was the danger that I would become a juvenile delinquent like a lot of the kids who spent time in the woods. These kids got JD cards by climbing the water tower and smoking cigarettes; and later, I'm sure, there would be sex and drugs in the woods, and not only people pulling their pants down to see if everyone came with the same standard issue parts. People strayed in the woods in a way they could not stray in a multipurpose room. But they also brought back riches—or at least I know that I, for one, brought back things that I would reach for all the rest of my life.

These days, I notice that many of the people I know, people of a certain class, want nothing more than that their children should be creative. Creativity! It is a holy word here in Cambridge, Massachusetts, one of the few things everyone would vote to increase if there were a referendum on the subject. My friends want their children to do much more than slavishly obey the rules of society. They want their children to hold on to their spirit of play; they want them to send off little flinty sparks of natural-born genius. And so they encourage their kids to study, but also to write poems and make jewelry, and to try their hand at batik. Will that work? Is that how children grow up to be creative—to be provided with kilns, and looms, and multipurpose rooms?

I don't know. Probably creativity, like intelligence, is a much crazier quilt than we realize; and probably some sorts of creativity do not depend on wandering past the skirts of society, out in unorganized territory, in the woods. Probably some sorts are not essentially wild. I hope that is true. For my husband and I do not live at the edge of the woods anymore; and the best we can do is provoke Luke with the luau room—a strange and extra, if all too supervised, space, in which he can carry on as he will when we are not carrying on ourselves.

## 2. THE DRIVEWAY

Additional provocation for Luke is the driveway, which is, even as I write, becoming a walled-in fruit garden of the Adam and

Eve type. We are planning espaliered pears, a sour cherry tree, blueberry bushes, raspberry bushes, gooseberry bushes. Strawberries. Other berries. A grape arbor, if we can keep the raccoons off it—this is a question. For our next-door neighbor has a grape arbor he grew for the leaves, and a lucky thing it is that his heart's interest is in dolmas. All summer, every night, an entire family of raccoons feasts on the grapes themselves. Is that what we want to happen to our grapes? And are we interested in hosting a summer-long block party?

We are not giving up our driveway in its entirety, God forbid. For here in the People's Republic of Cambridge, we have not only America's most creative snow plowers but also the country's most pitiless street cleaners. If in some future life, I had to pick a sound that evoked the experience of living here, in this place, in this now, it would be not the tolling of the bells in Harvard Yard, or the chatter of the neighborhood mockingbirds, or the bark of the vigilant Harry across the street, or even the all-too-frequent wail of someone's car or house alarm. It would be, without question, the familiar 7 A.M. blare of the street cleaners' advance guard, a bully of a vehicle with a giant public service speaker affixed to its small roof. STREET CLEANING: MOVE YOUR CAR TO THE OPPOSITE SIDE OF THE STREET OR YOUR CAR WILL BE TOWED. In Cambridge, you are always being towed for one reason or another; I am sure more people recognize the trucks from Pat's Towing than recognize the mayor. It is luxury indeed to have a driveway refuge. We would not think to give it up.

But we are able to make a fruit garden of our driveway and still have enough driveway for two cars because we started with a parking lot. Truly—our driveway looked as though it had been put down by someone who thrilled to blacktop, perhaps by the very inventor of asphalt himself. Or at least by someone who knew how to get a very good deal on paving. In any case, we have reclaimed the earth beneath it, and are turning it into a paradisical addendum to the luau room; and this, we think, will make us happy.

Is that what the asphalt enthusiast thought too? And how about the garage builder? That garage was put up for the ages. In the process of having its walls knocked out, it was for a time supported in one corner only by a single skinny pillar of cinderblocks. We worried that the roof was going to fall down. But the roof did not fall down; it did not even sag. And now that you can look up and witness all that once-hidden woodwork—it is clear why. What pleasure it must have given someone to get the roof to sit just so—to know it would forever overarch its cars, protecting and enshrining them.

What would he have thought if he had known that it would instead become part of this folly—this whatever? What if he had known it would fall into the hands of people who take their cars for granted—people who leave salt on their cars all winter, people who never used the garage anyway, being too lazy to unlock and unlatch and fold back the old vertical-fold doors, which stuck because the people were too lazy to oil them? Would he have wanted it to fall into the hands of people who proudly disdain the mechanical world? Who enjoy the word *hasp* but are only ninety-percent sure they know what it means?

Maybe he knew this would happen. For my husband and I are hardly alone in our urge to reshape and remake the world. Fellow Cantabrigians have turned their garages into apartments, libraries, cabanas, studios, offices, shops. They have put decks on top of them, hooked them up to their houses with catwalks. Friends have considered constructing a rooftop playground on theirs; I'm waiting for someone to install a carousel. For garage conversion is becoming a kind of art form in our town—so much so, that I can already see the Harvard University Press coffee-table book: *Great Garages! Vernacular Architecture in Cambridge, Massachusetts.*

We Cantabrigians are a vigorous lot, who think our vigor means something. That the individual has power; that transformation is possible; that people do not only inherit the world, but create it too. We can all spell hubris. Still, you may witness how buoyant is our human confidence by the worlds we have willed up out of the lumberyards. So many of us are self-made! We grapple with our pasts; we make projections about the future. What do we know, really? Never mind. We speak with aplomb: *We were once again not towed. Our families were dysfunctional. There is pectin in our future.*

## 3. MY GARAGE OF ORIGIN

We predict what people will say. My mother, for instance. *You are crazy!* Before she even came to see the luau-room-cum-Garden-of-Eden, I could hear her voice perfectly. *Where is the garage? I don't know where you get such crazy ideas!* And so on, and so on, when actually, I have garage renovation in the family.

For I grew up with a two-car garage, a good-sized space that wasn't big enough. We were a family with five kids, after all, and that meant ever-larger vehicles, culminating, when we were in high school, in Country Squires, with fake wood sides, and two-way back gates, and third seats from which you could wave at the people in the car behind yours. We did this on long trips that we now know to have been vacations—trips to the World's Fair, and Washington, D. C.—trips of which we can remember almost nothing except what went on in the car. Squabbles over who had to sit over the bump in the middle of the floor. Driving crises having to do with map-reading errors, and overheated radiators. Overheating was a general theme on these trips, which took place in the summer. For example, on one trip, my little brother's pet hamster overheated and died in the way back of the car. Who would have thought a hamster could have heat stroke? But this hamster did. Butterscotch was its name, and my little brother (now a father of twins who will soon want hamsters of their own) still reddens with emotion when he thinks of his first rodent. Who would have expected it would keel over when all the windows were open and my father was still asking for hot tea when we stopped?

But the hamster was from Greenacres Elementary. It was a class pet given to my brother to keep; and I know that when I, for one, thought about Butterscotch, I linked his frailty to his origin. Somehow it seemed not surprising that something from a school with a multipurpose room would not be able to survive life with us. Butterscotch was like many of our classmates, who were always talking about dying of the heat or the cold. They were not inured to things, the way we were in our family. Our family did not believe, back then, in air-conditioning. We believed that people who liked air-conditioning were soft. We believed that living with air-conditioning made you soft. We believed that we were tougher than other people, and not only poorer, as was obvious.

Now we think differently. Now my parents drive a silver Mercedes-Benz with climate control. Back then, we had only just graduated from VW Bugs, and Bugs still represented a kind of Platonic ideal. This was because the engine was in the back. My father once explained to us about how that gave the car good traction in the snow; and I remember vividly the one snowy day our car drove easily up a hill that had foiled a number of more impressive vehicles, no doubt outfitted with air-conditioning. VW's were feisty, like us, and we loved more than anything to pile out of ours, all seven of us, to the amazement of bystanders. (My two little brothers fit, back then, in what we called the box—the storage compartment behind the backseat.)

But of course, the day finally came when we could not fit all seven of us into a VW Bug; and then began the era of the ever-larger cars. We still had VW's as second cars. But our main cars were big cars—big cars requiring big-car storage. And so our grandest house project was conceived, the extension of the garage. This involved the installation of a steel beam, and the fashioning of a kind of half-height concrete nose out the front end of the garage, high enough to accommodate the hood of a car. It has been a success. The garage is now big enough for anything, a modern garage. It's true that it's a little difficult to judge when to stop when you can't see what's in front of the hood, but my father has fixed that. He's hung an old license plate just where the front end of the car should be; when you hit the license plate, you stop.

This is a typical Dad innovation—practical and simple, unlike the automatic door opener, which once came crashing down on a car roof by mistake. *American stuff,* my father commented as he surveyed the damage. *Fancy stuff.* We all shook our heads in disgust. But now the automatic door opener is as much a part of what we think of as home as the hanging-down license plates and the huge air conditioner in the den.

We are not what we were. When my mother came to Cambridge to see the luau room, what she actually said was, after a pause, "Very nice." My father observed that the old garage really was too small to use, just like our old garage in New York used to be. And then they sat down and made themselves comfortable, and admired the floor and the roof. They listened intently as I described how the storage shed was going to work. I ran into the house for tea, and came back prepared to explain everything else about the luau room too. About undesignated space, and creativity, and the possibility of transformation; about Cambridge culture, and the place of cars in our lives, and what fruit trees we were going to grow. I thought I would ease into the pig roast part of the luau plan, and make it clear that they would not be expected to attend.

But by then, my mother was reading the newspaper with great interest; and as for my father, he was stretched out and snoring, and looking most wonderfully at home.

## CLINT McCOWN

Memory.
It starts out innocently enough. You come upon a trail of bread crumbs in the woods and follow it. That simple. But the bread crumbs disappear behind you, and before long you're lost among the oldest trees, standing at a cottage door, with no choice left you but to knock.

The cottage, in this case, is in Fayetteville, Tennessee. The woods have thinned considerably, though the remnants are there. Hackberry and hawthorne trees shelter the upper side yard; giant sycamores and black locusts tower from the wild hedges at the back of the garden. The front yard is dotted with boxwoods, redbuds, dogwoods, and a few flowering hedges whose names I've never known. Also in front, near the buckled sidewalk, sits a single broad hickory stump, cut low to the ground, with rings to account for a hundred and seventy-five years—almost as long as my family has lived in this county.

The neighborhood, too, is old—a dead-end avenue with a scattering of weathered white houses, gray stone houses, brown stucco houses, most of them built before the days of garages. At the end of the street, at the top of the steep, short hill, is the county reservoir—the world's first gravitational water system, in fact, though you won't find any tourists here. It's a rugged place still, in spite of the houses, with prickly pears and briers, poison oak, hummingbirds and wild roses, red-thorned pyracanthas climbing over walls. Large ungroomed dogs roam freely but know which yards are theirs. On warm evenings when the heat has broken for the day, the pulsing whir of cicadas fills the trees.

The time is early summer, and I stand on the cracked, red concrete porch holding the storm door ajar, waiting for my cousin Ed to answer my knock. I can hear fierce whispers behind the walnut door and the sounds of frantic house-straightening.

A couple of wasps buzz disinterestedly above my head, and I notice several small gray nests wedged into the corners where the porch ceiling meets the house. Curls of sun-scorched paint peel from the frame around the door. I tug on a brittle strip, and it crumbles at my touch, leaving a fine, white powder on my fingers. The whole exterior needs painting. I've told Ed I will pay to have it done, but so far he hasn't got around to making the arrangements. I'll remind him again today; and if he'll give me the use of a broom, I'll knock down these nests before I go. I am the landlord, after all, and that means I have responsibilities.

To tell the truth, I had hoped Ed would be more help to me in handling those responsibilities. When he agreed to rent the place two years earlier, I felt relieved knowing that a relative was moving into my grandparents' old home. I thought I could count on him to spot the necessary repairs, bring in the workmen, and send me the bills. There were some things I just couldn't tend to myself, living, as I did, more than six hundred miles away.

But as I have now come to recognize, Ed and I differ greatly in what we consider necessary repairs. I did let him change the back bedroom into a laundry room, complete with new washer/dryer hookups. I bought him the deluxe ceiling fans he wanted, and even paid for a new interior paint job to cover up the paint job from the week before, because he didn't feel good about the color. And of course there was the new refrigerator, the kitchen wallpaper and linoleum, the new wiring and circuit-breaker box, and even a weekly yardman because Ed's back doesn't take well to mowing. But when the roof started to leak, he didn't mention it for a year—he just stuck a Styrofoam cooler on the mantelpiece until slugs started crawling down through the ruined plaster. When the protective weather panel broke off the side of the air conditioner in the rear bedroom, he never bothered to cover up the hole, but let an entire season of rain pour into the room until the floorboards warped and fungus sprouted in every corner. When vines began to grow into the house through the baseboards in the dining room, he never stepped outside to cut them down, because he thought they looked unusual spreading up the wall.

When I think about it, I guess Ed and I aren't all that closely related. We're connected in that Southern sense of family that stretches a web so vast and intricate that after a few generations people simply lose track of the particulars. In the peculiar language of genealogy, Ed and I are something like fifth cousins once removed, which is to say that neither of us knows which ancestor bound us into the same ongoing clan. But the kinship is there, nevertheless; and so he tolerates my constant hounding for the rent, and I tolerate his seldom paying it.

I didn't much mind this arrangement when Ed first moved in—he was unemployed then, and his second wife had just left him. But now he's the manager of a chain of all-night minimarts, and his third wife has a good job with the Redstone Arsenal in Huntsville. He just got back from two weeks at Disneyworld.

I learned about the Disneyworld trip when Ed called to explain about the problems that had developed in the house while they were gone. It seems the water heater exploded, flooding the cellar and ruining those of my grandmother's things that he had moved down there for storage. He needed the go-ahead for a new water heater. And wouldn't now be a good time to build an extra bathroom off the kitchen, and maybe a redwood deck for his barbecue.

I decided it was time to come and see things for myself. So here I am.

When Ed opens the door at last, we smile and shake hands. It's good to see him, regardless of the circumstances. I've known Ed all my life, and that weighs more than back rent and broken plaster. "Come on in," he says. "We were just cleaning the place up a little." But as I start to step into the living room, he stops me and points up to the top hinge of the storm door. "You know this door's about shot," he says. "I've tried new screws but they just won't hold. The hinge is stripped, and the thing's so old I doubt you could get the parts to replace it."

"I know," I tell him. "That top hinge has been a problem for years, for as long as I can remember. I'll go down and see about a new door this afternoon."

"I think that'd be a smart idea," Ed says. "The whole thing's in pretty bad shape."

"I don't know why we didn't replace it before now," I tell him. And then we move on into the house for the rest of the nightmare tour.

Later that day, making good on my promise, I drive down to Williams Lumber Company and order a new aluminum storm door, with self-storing windows, for a hundred and ten dollars. End of episode.

But the next day, when I'm sitting on the breezy back porch of my Uncle Hop's farmhouse, listening to relatives tell stories of their early days, a strange thing happens. My eighty-year-old Aunt Doris, who has already progressed through an account of the John Philip Sousa concerts she attended in her youth, begins a new story, about her girlhood on the farm. She tells us about being in the fields with her Papa one day when he was plowing. A large blacksnake, startled by the mule, fled in the wrong direction and was chopped apart by the plow. Then, she says, the segments of the snake came together again, and the repaired creature slithered away in the grass.

I've heard this folktale from other sources in other contexts, but never from the mouth of a believer. It amazes me that my own Aunt Doris, a retired nurse who knows the way a body works, could actually think her tale was true. Later, I challenge her on it, tell her that she knows as well as I do how impossible it is for any snake to do what she described.

"I can't help that," she tells me. "I remember it clear as day."

Right then, as if something has sprung wide open in my mind, I remember something, too, a childhood story of my own. It starts with the broken storm door on my grandparents' house, and the sudden recollection that the one who broke it years ago was me.

The year was 1958, and the month was early June. Storm doors were still something of a novelty in that part of the South. Most houses had screen doors, front and back—lightweight wooden frames covered with a rusting steel mesh. A child could burst through those doors without breaking stride, and without doing damage. But my grandfather always had an eye on progress, and when the new aluminum marvels came on the market, he bought one. I remember standing with my parents on that front porch—painted green in those days—listening to my grandfather enumerate the special features of the door: the safety-plate glass, the automatic compressor that eased the door shut without a slam, the locking mechanism, the adjustable tab for propping the door open at any angle. I was six years old and reasonably impressed. This was the first storm door I'd seen, and it gave me my first tangible proof that things in the modern world were always getting better.

Then the grown-ups went inside to join the other dinner guests and fix themselves drinks and talk about things they were happy to talk about, while I got permission to stay in the yard and play with my dog, a young German shepherd named Champ. I think it was Champ, though it might have been King, or Prince, or Sam, or Max. At one time or another I had German shepherds with all these names, and now time has distanced me so far from who they were that I can't recall which name attaches to which sad fate. Only the stark facts seem to have survived: one leapt into the back of a garbage truck and was crushed by the compressor; another was run over by a three-wheeled postal van; another wandered onto the highway and was hit by a tractor-trailer; one simply disappeared one night from beneath the kitchen table; and one ate strychnine that an old woman had left out for rats.

But I remember the dog itself, whatever the name, because it came into my life at that stage of childhood when a dog is the perfect accessory. We wandered every creek and patch of woods and unfenced yard. A free-roaming pair—though not like Timmy and Lassie, whom I'd already pegged as a pair of sentimental simps; more on the order of Rusty and Rin Tin Tin, those cavalry mascots who faced up to the hard edge of the world.

My mother, I remember, wanted me to rein him in, to teach him not to romp through other people's gardens and paw through their compost heaps. But what child wants to discipline a dog? So I never scolded him for ransacking garbage or digging under porches. I let him run wild.

No need to dwell on the boy-and-his-dog particulars of that afternoon in my grandparents' yard—the scene is too clichéd already, riddled with false sentiment. That's the trouble with archetypal imagery: it ultimately lies. No single image can endure in life; other moments crowd onstage, and for better or worse, image always gives way to narrative, to story lines we might never have looked for.

I left Champ in the yard and went inside to watch television for half an hour before dinner. In clear weather we could pick up two fuzzy channels—the Huntsville and Nashville stations. The picture was grainy and gray; often it rolled like broken film, and sometimes we would lose the horizontal hold and the screen would become a tangle of live debris, unrecognizable as anything worth staring at. But I stared anyway, and listened, and wiggled the rabbit ears of the antenna until something came on. This time it was Marshal Matt Dillon in *Gunsmoke*. I don't remember the episode, but I do seem to remember everything else: the slant of sunlight coming through the glass of the new storm door, the scratchy mat of carpet against my elbows and knees, the smell of fried chicken, the laughter and light conversation of the grown-ups in the dining room behind me.

Then from outside, down the hill, came the frantic yelping of the dog. I stood and looked through the storm door's sparkling glass in time to see him race past the boxwood at the lower corner of the yard. He saw me, too, and tore madly up the sidewalk toward the porch. I knew at once he wouldn't stop, but there was no way to head him off. I yelled his name—yes, it was Champ, after all—and watched him leap headlong into the shatterproof glass. His body crumpled and fell; for a split second I thought he'd broken his neck. But he was up at once, as if he hadn't felt the blow at all, and dashed from the porch to the yard, still howling. There was clearly something wrong.

By now the grown-ups were hurrying into the room. "Better grab the boy," someone said. It was Big Jim Wakefield, a burly, good-natured man who breathed as if he were always out of breath and moved like a bear. He and his wife, Jane, had four sons of their own, decent boys, and he guessed before anyone else the move I was likely to make. But he spoke too late, and before my father could reach me I bolted for the door. I hit it at full speed, just as Champ had done; but I was coming from the proper side, and the aluminum frame shot back against its hinges and stuck open against the white wood siding of the house. In that simple moment, the hinge was irreparably popped, and the door would never work perfectly again.

"Stay clear of that dog," my grandfather called after me. "He might be rabid." That was a standard refrain in those days, because the county was full of rabid animals—foxes, bats, raccoons, squirrels, possums, and sometimes dogs. I knew Champ wasn't rabid, but the specter of hydrophobia slowed me anyway. Like every child my age, I knew the standard test for rabies. If Champ did bite me for some reason, they would have to cut off his head and send it away for examination. I stopped in the center of the front lawn; Champ blurred past me twice, then veered away into the upper side yard and began a wild race back and forth along the length of the lot, as if he thought he could outrun what was happening to him.

"He's mad all right," someone else said—a red-faced man named Raymond who brought me stuffed animals on his visits.

By now my father had swooped me back to the porch. My grandmother, my mother, and Jane Wakefield were just emerging from the house, their tumblers of Jack Daniel's still in their hands. My grandmother lit a cigarette and in a low voice said to my grandfather, "Clinton, you'd better get your gun." He disappeared into the house.

"That's a good precaution," Jim Wakefield said, and he lumbered across the yard to the trunk of his Buick and took out a twelve-gauge shotgun. Jane Wakefield put an arm around my shoulder and hugged me. "I'm sorry, Sugar," she said. "But maybe everything will turn out fine."

By the time Jim Wakefield got back to the porch, my grandfather had returned with his pistol, and my father and Raymond had their guns out as well. It seems strange to me now, but in Fayetteville in those days every man I knew kept a firearm nearby. Guns were central to the culture, and always had been. This was, after all, the town where Andrew Jackson had quartered his troops for the Creek Indian Wars; where Davy Crockett and Sam Houston had spent time as teenagers; where Frank James once shot a man dead on the courthouse lawn.

Raymond was a policeman, and he carried a thirty-eight-caliber revolver; so did my father, who in those days was an agent for the Alcohol and Tobacco Tax Unit of the Treasury Department—revenuers, they were called—and his job was to track moonshiners through the mountains. Beside them stood my grandfather with his nine-shot twenty-two pistol, the gun he took to poker games—because my grandfather was a gambler who didn't always play with friends. On any other occasion I might have been armed myself—at the age of six I already owned a lever-action air rifle and was allowed to go hunting on my own. I'd even been shot once myself, by an older boy who put a pellet in my backside for fun.

But as we stood there on the porch—the men with their weapons drawn, my grandmother calmly smoking her cigarette, Jane and my mother both gripping me by the shoulders— Champ suddenly turned and charged toward us. For a moment everyone froze, and I saw that Jim Wakefield had a bead on Champ with his twelve-gauge. "Don't," I said. Jim was a good shot—he could knock down twenty quail in an afternoon and never miss—and I knew if he pulled the trigger Champ would be dead before his nose hit the ground. But he didn't shoot; he swung the barrel skyward, said, "Oh hell," and leaped off the porch into a boxwood. At that almost everyone scrambled for cover, jumping over lawn furniture and climbing onto the concrete ledges of the porch's broad support columns. Only my grandmother and I stood our ground, and Champ raced right between us, snapping his jaws, but not biting. He crossed the length of the porch, then veered again into the front yard, where he began to run in smaller, slower circles.

"He's not mad," my grandmother said. "But I believe he's been poisoned." As she said this, Champ finally collapsed onto his side, but he continued snapping his jaws and clawing at the grass. We all moved down into the yard and formed a circle around him, with me nearest his head. His eyes fixed on me with a sense of recognition, and he began to crawl toward me; but my grandfather eased me a couple of steps backward and said, "We still can't get too close."

Jim Wakefield eased the butt of his gun to the ground and said to my father, "It's a shame what needs to be done."

"It is a shame," Jane said, and took her husband's arm.

But for a while my father didn't answer, and we all just stood there looking at the dog until it went into convulsions. "It's your choice," my father said; and I didn't have to look up to know he was talking to me.

I knew what I was supposed to say. When you're raised around guns, part of the catechism is not to let animals suffer. It's my guess, though, that I told them to leave Champ alone. A dog in pain has got a better chance than one who's dead, and I don't think any child can believe in death as a form of mercy. But I really don't know what I told them, because after the image of my

grandfather pointing his pistol down at Champ's head and looking to me for instructions, the memory flies apart like broken
crockery.

Maybe that's not too hard to figure. Watching the dog writhe
away its final few minutes, whimpering and coughing up blood,
or approving the bullet my grandfather might have blasted
through its brain—either option could have been too much for
me to handle. Maybe my weakness then still keeps me from remembering now.

But maybe there's another reason. Maybe whatever it is that
portions out the past and stores it in secret pockets of the mind
has a power to make even routine choices with a wisdom we're
not conscious of. Throw this out, it's useless; save that, you'll need
it. Maybe my memory hasn't saved the moment of the dog's
death because that moment isn't central to the scene.

I do, however, remember the epilogue. My grandfather
fetched Dr. McRady from across the street, who crouched over
the dog for a few moments and then said he thought it was a case
of strychnine poisoning. Jim Wakefield took a burlap feed sack
from the trunk of his car and spread it on the grass. My father
lifted the carcass by the leather collar and the tail and laid it on
the burlap. Then he and my grandfather picked the whole thing
up and eased it onto the floor of the backseat of our Plymouth.
I got in back with the dog, my father and grandfather climbed
into the front, and we drove out to a familiar stretch of woods at
the southern end of the county. I waited in the car—by order,
not choice—while they carried the body away through the trees
for burial. Only now do I realize, in my reconstruction of the
scene, that they were not gone long enough, had not actually

buried the dog but must have merely dumped it in the under-growth.

When we got back home, a friend of mine from two houses down was standing in our yard throwing cane spears at the hickory tree. His name was Rex Holt, and he was a year older than me, a rough kid, but not too mean. "I heard about your dog," he said. "Tough luck."

Sometime later, a week or a month, I moved on to other dogs—to Prince, and King, and Sam, and Max—and each of them in turn came to an unfortunate end. But Champ's is the fate that lingers most vividly. It's been more than thirty-five years now, but memory can still put me right back in that scene and conjure up emotions as immediate as yesterday.

They aren't the same emotions, though. While the original child grieved for himself and his unlucky pet, the child I re-create through recollection has a different burden, all his own. That child knows the future. He is a storehouse of epilogues—and as he looks at the people around him in the evening light, he wishes he could save them from what he knows. He can't, of course. In memory we are hearts without voices, and cannot say the simplest things.

And so he stands there mute, with the knowledge that his grandfather will die this month of a stroke; that Raymond will soon be shot through the heart by a bank robber; that Jim Wakefield will drive his Buick over a cliff; that Jane Wakefield will kill herself with her husband's shotgun; that Dr. McRady will die in a nursing home; that Rex Holt for unknown reasons will blow himself up with a case of dynamite; that his grandmother will succumb to emphysema; that his mother will lose a fight with cancer; and that his father will contract a brain disease that eats holes in the memory.

A dog's death doesn't mean much in this world.

And yet it does, because without it I might have no frame to set these people in, no means to call them all together at a place in time. Dog is no longer dog, but triggering device.

Still, I can't help being skeptical of what's been triggered. Memories fade like photographs; time bleaches out subtleties so that even the sharpest distinctions become blurred. If we stare at a familiar sight while darkness falls, the image may cloud over but we still believe we know what's there. So the mind compensates: imagination fills in all the gaps of a failing vision, plasters over the webwork of cracks in memory's wall. Such imaginative restoration is an ongoing process, and sooner or later any memory might be more imagination than true recollection, more patchwork than original wall.

And so my Aunt Doris truly remembers a blacksnake that did not die beneath the plow, but resegmented itself and escaped through the grass. And in the power of that vision, she holds as well the image of her father walking behind a mule on a certain day in a certain field, maybe with the sun striking his face at a certain angle, or the wind blowing his hair, or his arm reaching out to her. In this way only, he remains unlost.

It could be that much of what I now remember belongs to the world of Aunt Doris's unsevered blacksnake. If I were with her now, I wouldn't balk at such unlikely details, but would ask her to tell me more about that remarkable day in a young girl's life when the laws of nature were suspended. But time has leapt ahead once more: it's now a new spring, and the world has changed again. My cousin Ed has left town, and I suppose is now promising rent to a brand-new landlord. The house sits empty, and though I don't feel good about it, I've put it up for sale. So far no one seems interested. Buyers tend to go with first impressions, and I guess the peeling paint still overshadows the new storm door.

Aunt Doris died in January. When I remember our last conversation, I find myself wishing I could remember it differently, and I play out alternate versions in my mind, replastering that wall even before the cracks have begun to show. I know now how memory works. Someday, years from now, looking back, I will remember Aunt Doris telling me about her blacksnake; and in that memory I'll nod my head and say, "Yes, I believe you." And for all I know, it will be the absolute truth.

## BAILEY WHITE

A Garden is a lovesome thing, God wot!
　　Rose plot,
　　Fringed pool,
　　Ferned grot—
　　The veriest school
　　Of Peace; and yet the fool
Contends that God is not—
Not God! in Gardens! when the eve is cool?
Nay, but I have a sign:
'Tis very sure God walks in mine.
　　　　　　　　*—Thomas Edward Brown*

Clink, clunk, clink. Day after day that summer they could hear the little taps of the chisel as Nana carved those words into a slab of marble out in the new garden she was making on the side of the house. By August the carving was done, little wobbly letters with mismatched serifs crawling across the pink marble slab.

That winter she planted two little tea olive trees at the entrance to the garden, and the rose plot from the poem—Lady Banksia, Dainty Bess, Cecil Brunner, and Seven Sisters around a bronze sundial.

The next summer was rainy, but she dug a round hole in the mud and planted pickerelweed around the edge, and that was the fringed pool.

The next spring, her skills in cement honed by the work she

had done the year before lining the pool in the drizzling rain, she tackled the ferned grot, and ended up in September with a slumping concrete dome with arched openings on four sides, studded with broken conch shells she picked up at the Gulf. "Like fossils from an ancient seabed," she told them intently, brushing the sand from her fingers in little twiddling motions.

The ferns began to thicken and spread, the roses bloomed, and the tea olive trees were shoulder high. Nana laid little flagstone paths in artistic curves connecting the different features of the garden, bordered with Ophiopogon, and organized garden tea parties for her granddaughters. She dressed them up in white lawn and black stockings and tried to get them to assume graceful poses on the sloping concrete benches in the ferned grot, teacup in one hand, saucer in the other. But mosquitoes swarmed out of the fringed pool, the black wool stockings were prickly and tight, and they didn't like hot tea.

"My God, woman," their grandfather roared down from the house. "What the hell is a grot?"

Then the tea party was over, cups hastily set down with relief, mosquito bites scratched at last, and one granddaughter poked her sister and whispered, "God wot!" With a chorus of giggles the granddaughters trooped back to the house, ignoring the graceful curving path and stomping over the Ophiopogon border. And Nana, in tears, was left to gather up the pieces of a broken cup.

Years went by; the tea olive trees grew up and formed a canopy over the garden entrance, and the ferns took off and spread into the bog behind the garden formed by the leaky pool. In the 1940s the roof collapsed on the grot, and it actually took on the look of some kind of ruin. Nana became more and more a figure of fun to her family as she aged. "God wot" evolved in the family linguistics into an expletive, and surrounded as she was by irreverent loved ones, Nana's sanity began to ebb. She was always brushing imaginary grains of sand off her fingers, and she thought that flowers were in bloom out of season.

"Oh, dearest!" she would gush on a dreary January afternoon, gesturing with twiddling fingers to the bleak, stubbly lawn, her eyes filling with tears. "Oh, dearest . . . the lilies!"

"God wot, woman!" her husband would growl, glaring at her from under his bushy eyebrows. "Can't you see it's the dead of winter? Ain't no lilies blooming out of that cold ground!"

In the 1950s the garden took over its own management. The more delicate Cecil Brunner and Dainty Bess succumbed to black spot, but the Seven Sisters grew into a mat over the sundial, and the Lady Banksia climbed out of the garden and up into the tops of the pine trees. The ferns choked out the pickerelweed, and a race of giant black-and-red grasshoppers bred in the Ophiopogon borders.

Ida, one of the tea-drinking granddaughters, had inherited her grandmother's interest in botany, without the sentiment, and made a serious study of several species of indigenous rice. One summer Ida dug out the ferns that had taken over the half-acre bog behind the pool and planted rows of little rice plants there. It was a constant struggle to keep the ferns from taking back the bog, but in one year the rice grew to towering clumps. In the fall Ida gathered a bushel of it, shaking the grains out of the drooping heads. But she found it almost impossible to separate the grain from the husk. The winnowing method she set up on the porch with screen wire and a fan wasn't up to it. The husk, with its sharp little backward-facing barbs, clung tenaciously to the grain, and it needed many picking fingers to do the job. But Ida's children were no more interested in hulling rice than Ida herself had been at their age in Victorian tea parties, and the rice clumps went unharvested in the bog behind the garden, reseeding themselves year after year.

In the fall of 1968 Ida's son Louis went off to college and came home for his spring break with a new enthusiasm for gardening and many questions for Ida about the pH scale and dolomite lime. He spent days behind the garden, putting in drains and digging manures into the old rice field. On a hot afternoon in early September he took Ida for a walk through the old overgrown garden.

"I want to show you something," he told her.

They stopped behind the rubble-strewn grot, and Ida looked out over what used to be her rice plantation. "What is that?" she said. "Palmate leaves, edges dentate—it reminds me of Rose of Sharon, but this square stem, like a mint. An odd smell for a plant, and these dense, gummy flower clusters. What are you growing here, Louis?"

"It's not Rose of Sharon," said Louis. Then he showed her his drying racks in the grot, and together they snipped off several bristling bundles of flowers. They sat on a bench near the roses, and Louis rolled a thin little yellow cigarette.

"This is against the law," said Ida, squinting her eyes and taking a little puff. Still, she thought, remembering the backward-facing barbs on every grain of rice, how can a thing be wicked when it is so easy to harvest? She lay back on the bench and closed her eyes. Little red pinpoints of light spread and burst into sparkles.

"God wot!" said Ida.

"Yeah," said Louis.

The summer day seemed to swell and ebb.

"There's a bronze sundial under those Seven Sisters," said Ida.

"Yeah," said Louis.

"I broke a teacup here once," said Ida.

"Yeah," said Louis.

The next afternoon a little propeller airplane flew low over the house, dipping and circling. That night Ida and Louis pulled up every one of the plants and threw them over the fence to the cows. All night there was that rhythmic munch, munch, munch, and when the airplane came back in the morning there was nothing left but a few straggling rice plants, starved for sunlight, and three sweet-faced Jersey cows snuffling their wet noses against the fence.

In the 1970s Louis's sister Della rode the bus out to California and married a poet. But she grew homesick, and she lured her husband back across the continent with poetical descriptions of Gulf breezes and the green evening mists in her great-grandmother's old garden. They planted a little eucalyptus tree behind the roses, a memento of California, Della went to work in the family feed mill, and Ida cleared out a space in a back room, where old guns were stored, for the California poet. But the damp and heat didn't agree with him, and no one understood his work.

"Nice-looking young fellow Della brought back from California."

"Calls himself a poet."

"That's a real poetical family out there. I remember old Miss Anna carving out that poem, something about a garden."

"Sure did, chipped every letter out of a slab of marble she got down at the monument shop. Took her a whole summer."

"This California boy, though, he writes his on paper. Uses a typewriter, I believe."

"Yeah, well, that ain't quite the same thing, now is it?"

When the poet broke out in prickly heat rash at the end of his second August, it was the last straw, and he packed his typewriter up and headed back out west. The eucalyptus tree, however, got its roots down into the septic tank drain field and within three years it was towering over the garden, shedding great ragged slabs of bark in the fringed pool and breaking Della's heart with the clean, sharp smell of her California love.

In the 1980s people all over the country stopped eating eggs and beef because of the cholesterol scare, and the feed mill shut down. The mysterious tapping sounds they had been attributing to ghosts in the attic turned out to be drops of rainwater leaking through the roof and hitting the ceiling, and the plumbing backed up because the roots of the eucalyptus tree had clogged up the antique red clay pipes that formed the septic tank drain field. The roofer came down out of the attic shaking his head, and the plumber came up from behind the garden saying "Uh, uh, uh."

In 1987 the house was sold to a hotel and restaurant corporation. Within three months it was replumbed, rewired, reroofed, and repainted. A bulldozer leveled the grot and filled in the rice bog. In one day a team of professional gardeners hacked through the tangle of roses and ferns with weed eaters and chain saws until they came down to the old winding paths, the sundial, and the poem on its marble slab. They trimmed the opening under the tea olive trees into a neat arch, they replaced the rampant Lady Banksia and Seven Sisters with modern, controllable roses, they patched the pool and installed a recirculating filter pump with a spray fountain and a bronze nymph, and they edged the Ophiopogon borders. In the ferns, where the grot had been, they put a teak Chinese Chippendale-style bench with a potted topiary tree rosemary at each end.

In 1990, to commemorate its opening as a country inn, the house and its garden were featured on the cover of *Leisure South* magazine. In April, when the roses came into bloom, the magazine editor and photographer came down from Atlanta. She was feeling weary of her job—the endless articles she would write in the magazine's relentlessly jaunty style about redecorating family rooms and putting up redwood fences. He was feeling bitter. On the long drive from the airport he showed her a photograph he had taken at a New Year's celebration in Chinle, Arizona—an old man and an old woman dancing, their eyes closed, both his big lumpy hands clasped behind her fat bulging back. In the background glittery things shimmered out of the blackness.

"This is my *Moonrise over Hernandez*," he said.

They stood for a minute in the shade of the two tea olive trees and looked into the sunny garden. "And here I am at another goddamned garden, another goddamned dewdrop on another goddamned rose, more of that goddamned green murk in the background."

He stepped out into the sunlight and went to work, not quite focusing on a full-blown Tropicana rose, catching a rainbow in the spray behind the nymph, zooming in on a tiger swallowtail on a potted red geranium.

"What's this," she said. "It might be a gravestone." She ran her fingers along the eroded lines of spidery letters. "We could do one of those rubbings," she said, squinting to read the words. "Something about a garden, God something, rose something. Here it says when something is cool, eve, when the eve is cool."

But it was hot in the sun on that April day, and she sat down on the teak bench in the shade and thought up titles for articles she might write. "Chintz Transforms a Foyer," "Lighten That Hedge with Old-Fashioned Elaeagnus!"

She lay back on the bench and closed her eyes. She could hear the clicks and whirrings of his cameras like little bird songs. Through her eyelids she could see shifting patterns of sun and shade.

"Imagine," she said, "this garden being here, unchanged, all these years."

"Yep," he said, stuffing rolls of film into the pockets of his vest. "Well, that's what we like about the South."

"Still," she said, "let's just sit here a minute, in the shade, in this peaceful place."

# ALLAN GURGANUS

H enry James, who knew a great deal, if not everything, considered these two words the most perfectly beautiful in English: "summer afternoon." My own favorite since childhood is just "Home." I love the way its stately gate of an "H" swings open onto the shielded domesticity of roundnesses, the way Home's little "e" stands, back-looking, bye-saying, like the household's child sent out to wave company safe into the night. That last sentence, playing house with the letters of one word, shows both my novelist's trade—making something of seemingly nothing much—and the reason my rooms look like they do— that overloaded, overheated alphabet, my home.

Good taste interests me mostly for the human exceptions it can make. My rule-bending tendency makes me wonder how the houses shown in magazines manage their Zen cleanliness.

Where do such houses store, for instance, the many previous magazines full of houses like themselves? I always intend to live simply, in stark white rooms scary with elegant rectitude: a futon, a lacquer table, one ripening persimmon, and a vase bearing, say, a single twig. I manage that till the following morning, on the sidewalk waiting for the garbagemen, there's this Deco-ish thirties rattan chaise in almost-perfect shape that must really come home and help home become more fully Home. Within one week and three more finds I've gone from Buddhist purity to Santa's workshop. Oh, well.

When I lived in New York, a real estate ad might have described my lair as a one-bedroom apartment with a balcony. How partial all truths are. I worked there because—given Manhattan's office rents—I couldn't afford a home away from home. Those of us involved in cottage industries must pay especially industrious attention to the cottage itself. This economic necessity—the keeping of desk near bed near fridge, this mingling of love, work, and the usual eat/sleep—comes to feed the writing, becomes a joy that lets me live with my research—known in some circles as clutter. The apartment was then, as is my place now, as is any place I live, a provincial museum of my collections motley and grand, it is a file drawer with a bed in it. It's a rescue-mission halfway house for objects equidistant between being fashionable and extinct. Over time, alongside my fiction, the rent-controlled apartment evolved, grew peony-layered with allusions and jokes. Where I live becomes partly office supply store, partly a tragicomic thrift shop attempt at creating a little bourgeois comfort, partly alchemist's medicine chest, partly the toy-strewn nursery of a well-equipped if not quite spoiled child. The place also serves as a Southerner's ancestor-worship altar, a hermit's cave, a telephone clearinghouse, and, whenever possible, a seducer's den. Mostly it's a beloved yeasty petri dish for ideas, friendships, hopes. It is Yeats's "rag and bone shop of the heart."

Six days a week, for seven years, I paced and mumbled in those rooms, finishing my novel *Oldest Living Confederate Widow Tells All.* The book, 719 pages long, offers the voice of one ninety-nine-year-old woman, a veteran of the last veteran of our Civil War, somebody "too old to lie, too vain to need to." The novel covers 150 years of dark American comedy; it also covered every square inch of the research-site apartment. Bathroom walls were paved with tintypes showing doomed boy soldiers whose clear eyes seem to know. I am still addicted to the bedroom's images of Lincoln's messianically human mud pie of a face. (I've heard that Picasso had a collection of Lincolnalia; Marilyn Monroe considered Lincoln the sexiest man in American history, and she married Arthur Miller because of his Lincolnly length.) But where was I? Oh yes, underfoot crumbles one informative 1888 Montgomery Ward catalogue, a useful gauge to the daily objects of home back then.

Between projects, I mostly collect what most collects me. My two hundred masks become tacit company for any novel's long haul; masks offer an anthology of squints, a laughing Hogarthian audience, a crop of fellow souls trapped in some amicably melancholy plaster-polychromed limbo. They are co-sufferers, co-jokes. The masks range from fifteenth-century French altar carvings to wonders made by my father and brothers and a cross-stitched sampler by Mom: THOUGHTFUL DEEDS BRING HAPPINESS—I sure hope so. These rest among a plentiful supply of last Halloween's choicest Woolworth's luridness.

Oscar Wilde warned against people who understand the

price of everything and the value of nothing. In our trumped-up lucre-lusting age, taste is everywhere, minus meaning, robbed of the contradictory, the compassionate, the personal. (If "home" is the most roundly pure of English words, what is "homeless"?) In such a time, home—as in the 1820s to '40s—again seems Biedermeier-reified, half holy. We are sensible to try perfecting what little space we do control. I am personally untrustfunded while engaged in a profession that pays, if at all, only fitfully. I have access only to values, prices being lately so pricey. And that, I've come to believe, is not so bad a deal.

I have one table where I write; another is reserved for a recent pleasure—trying to illustrate my fiction. The writing desk is meted and humanized by four to fifteen clocks, all in working order—a middle-class point of honor. These serve as mementos mori, as metronomic counterpoint to reading my work aloud, plus they're the source of Eastern Standard Time, which lets a guy know when he can finally knock off after a hard day's truthful lying on the page. A recent favorite timepiece is a four-foot ashwood Deco, one that for fifty years ran a Glens Falls, New York, public grammar school's bell system; every day at 3:10 P.M., the whole mechanism still shudders with orgiastic knock-kneed release. (My reader and guest here, matter remembers!) The black lacquer-bronze-onyx Art Nouveau mantel clock belonged to my grandmother, who brought it from Edinburgh in the 1880s to boomtown Chicago. Every time this item sounds forth its blurry Westminster gongs, whether I consciously hear them or not, I am instantly realigned with all the decades that have plaited through its workings, in rooms as stubbornly improvised and determinedly shabby-genteel as mine here.

If clocks play abstracted headmistresses to the writing table, old photos convene an undistracting reunion here on the table where I draw. Family pictures show forebears both genetic and literary—actual great-grandpops stand alongside Dr. Chekhov, who perhaps more deeply and daily, *is* one. The table's ivory telephone was salvaged from a 1920s Harlem brothel—two blocks from the Cotton Club—and, I'm told, a four-star house is not a home. The imagined story of what was ordered through this receiver via room service gives mundane phone talks a certain buttery and jazzed allure.

With a novel regularly brewing among such die-hard character-burdened things, a cross-pollination goes on: the book expands into the background that home provides, and homey totems sometimes insist on foreground rights. Things unionize. They demand walk-on roles within the novel.

You know how in dreams you find familiar objects employed on unexpected errands? The hairbrush is a weapon, your misplaced address book becomes Saint Peter's guest ledger. That same upgrading distortion can send beloved items into your book's daily dreamed growth. But first let me ask you to name the three things you'd save first from any disaster at home. Hard, isn't it? I'd now ask you to tell the story of why those three. Why should those stories make those storied objects mean more to you than things of greater seeming value?

Before I show you my homey clocks, Pygmalioned and ticking into fiction, a last element needs explaining: an 1830s life-size Italian wood and plaster saint with whom I've lived some years in concord and in sin (her concord, my sin). I found Saint Ursula at a Manhattan street fair. It was a summer afternoon, one as sensually perfect as its name is euphonious. Amidst junk far beneath her, Ursula, eyes aimed heavenward, was being remartyred—this go-round on the pyres of commerce, poor underrated thing.

Most of us know the feeling of being deeply summoned by some exquisite object, exquisite at least to you. The price of ignoring its call? That damnation named: eternal regret. Sometimes you get a crawling before you even see the necessary thing. Then you turn, and the certainty is nearly as pure as that the disciples must have felt in leaving their tools of trade and following, luggageless. For me it sometimes sets in as a sort of aural buzz, high-pitched as owner's whistle call to dog. Other times, a smell foretells nearby delight, the scent part metal, part celestial freesia. That June I saw this life-size woman, impossibly fine, a piece of ecclesiastical processional statuary, pearl-like in her splendid masochism, hardly a Bernini but all the more poignant for that saintly failing. My first glance told me this: "We will go home by cab." I ran across the street and milked the nearest cash machine half dry and then—eureka—after lugging her toward a cab, was suddenly seated alongside an actual saint. We drew looks from pedestrians. The driver—one rearview mirror's matched set of puffy eyes—finally croaked in a voice jaded yet endlessly bemused as Manhattan itself. "You had to have it, right?" He understood. Grateful, I nodded. I surrendered then (the cabbie wouldn't mind). I lightly rested my head on her shoulder; her plaster there was warm because this was a summer afternoon. Home we went. I overtipped the driver. "Bye, doll," he called back at sixty mph. I love New York.

Here is how Ursula and the clocks got into my novel. I don't know which of them started it or how they did so, but a charac-

ter in there began looking a lot like Ursula. Lady More Marsden
is a comically self-involved slave owner and pianoforte whiz, mistress of a two-thousand-acre plantation. The Lilacs. Of all white
ladies near Falls, North Carolina, in the 1860s, she is locally perhaps the whitest: "She had the oval saintliness of a very hard-
boiled egg. Her freed slaves—thirty-odd years after Sherman's
fire darkened her—claimed Lady hadn't been all that bad. Hob-
bies kept her clear of the worst mischief: pianoforte, knitting,
doing jigsaw puzzles of European vistas, and, naturally, fainting.
Plus the clocks. Her mansion's seventy-odd rooms each housed
a novelty clock—marble, bronze, quartz. All showed subjects
from mythology. Swans mounted Leda ladies every quarter hour,
tiring. Hercules' flat tummy was a walleyed German pocket
watch. Under Phaëthon's chariot, pendulums swung, cheery as
the hearts of peasants, solemn as famous necessary manly parts.
Lady Marsden, in a white silk wrapper, hand-cranked every cloi-
sonné Apollo herself. 'Somebody has to.' Thursday—the day that
gears wound down—Lady would actually rise before noon, she'd
string an opera jailer's worth of keys around her neck. She'd tug
on a green visor purchased from Falls's one pawnbroker. 'Something about it appealed to me.' Mrs. Marsden laughed at her own
paleness tinted fishy green and off she'd scuff to wind parlor's
seven-day-movement masterpieces. She'd taken a two-year cor-
respondence course in horology. Slaves made fun of the word,
though they knew their mistress's chastity was total, dull. Strange
that neighbors brought the usually helpless Lady their stalled
locket watches. She worked in her high ivory four-poster, visor
tugged low, black eyepiece screwed into her all but albino face.
Favorite tools: sterling sugar tongs and her eyebrow tweezers."

Fiction's imaginative markup. Using what's at hand, I, like

you, live in my own workshop, putting this over there, trying that over here, a little to the left. My rooms are stuffed with what's seemingly semiworthless, with the chipped, the tired-of-being-whimsical. You might think I've opened an orphanage for cast-off images, has-been bibelots, but those of us who hear the siren song of old things, new things, things damaged or unfinished, understand that we do not choose them any more than we can consciously pick those lovely worthless human paragons love makes us love. The few true things adopt us. The choicest things you've acquired—be they inherited, store-bought or street—prove once and for all: "inanimate object" is a contradiction in terms. Matter matters.

Earlier I asked what three items you would save from your home, fast. And, friend, in case of fire, know this—if they could move and weren't weighted by the awful burden of immortality that you and I have been lightly spared, you are the first thing those three would save. I believe, to them, the sight of you means welcome, happiness, and use. For your own storied objects, you remain the sun, the organizing principle, the godlike visiting myth.

For your relics, you are home. Therein lies a tale. . . .

LYNDA BARRY was born in Richland Center, Wisconsin. She grew up in Seattle and now lives in Evanston, Illinois. A winner of the Washington State Governor's Award, she is the creator of the nationally syndicated cartoon strip, Ernie Pook; a commentator for National Public Radio; and an acclaimed playwright (*The Good Times Are Killing Me*). She is also the author of *Girls & Boys; Big Ideas; Naked Ladies, Naked Ladies, Naked Ladies; Everything in the World; Down the Street; The Fun House; Come Over, Come Over; My Perfect Life;* and *It's So Magic.*

RICHARD BAUSCH is the author of six novels, including *Rebel Powers* and *Violence,* as well as three collections of stories: *Spirits & Other Stories, The Fireman's Wife & Other Stories,* and *Rare & Endangered Species.* His novel, *The Last Good Time,* was released as a motion picture in 1995. He has won two National Magazine awards, a Guggenheim Fellowship, a Lila-Wallace *Reader's Digest* Fund Writer's Award, and the Award of the American Academy of Arts & Letters. He was born in Fort Benning, Georgia, and resides in Fauquier County, Virginia, with his family.

TONY EARLEY is the author of the short story collection *Here We Are in Paradise.* His stories have appeared in *Harper's, TriQuarterly, Best American Short Stories,* and *New Stories from the South.* He has won a PEN Syndicated Fiction prize and a National Magazine award. Raised in Rutherfordton, North Carolina, he lives with his wife in Ambridge, Pennsylvania.

JAMES FINN GARNER grew up in Dearborn, Michigan. He is the author of *Politically Correct Bedtime Stories, Once Upon a More Enlightened Time,* and *Politically Correct Holiday Stories.* His work has appeared in *Playboy,* the *Wall Street Journal, Chicago Tribune Magazine, Chicago Reader,* and *The Nose.* He lives in Chicago with his family.

HENRY LOUIS GATES, JR., was born and raised in Mineral County, West Virginia. He was graduated summa cum laude from Yale with a degree in history, and he was a London correspondent for *Time* magazine before receiving his Ph.D. in English from Cambridge University. He writes frequently for such publications as *Harper's, The New York Times Book Review, The New Yorker,* and *The Village Voice.* His books include *Figures in Black, The Signifying Monkey* (for which he received an American Book Award), *Loose Canon,* and *Colored People,* a memoir. He is now Professor of English and Chairman of Afro-American Studies at Harvard University.

ALLAN GURGANUS was born in Rocky Mount, North Carolina, and now lives in Chapel Hill. He is the author of *The Oldest Living Confederate Widow Tells All,* which won the Sue Kaufman Prize for Best First Fiction; *White People,* which won the *Los Angeles Times* Book Prize; and the just-published *Recent American Saints.*

COLIN HARRISON grew up in Philadelphia and is a graduate of Haverford College and the University of Iowa's Writers' Workshop. He is the author of two novels, *Break and Enter* and *Bodies Electric.* He is Deputy Editor of *Harper's Maga-*

*zine.* He lives in New York City with his wife, Kathryn, and their two children.

KATHRYN HARRISON was born and raised in Los Angeles, California. A graduate of Stanford University and of the University of Iowa's Writers' Workshop, she recently received a fellowship from the New York Foundation for the Arts. She is the author of the novels *Thicker Than Water* (a *New York Times* Notable Book of 1991), *Exposure* (also a *New York Times* Notable Book and a national best-seller), and the recently published *Poison.* She lives in New York City with her husband, Colin, and their two children.

GISH JEN was born in Queens, New York. She is the author of the novel *Typical American,* which was shortlisted for the National Book Critics' Circle Award. Her short stories have appeared in *The Atlantic* and *The New Yorker,* as well as numerous anthologies, including *The Heath Anthology of American Literature* and *Best American Short Stories.* Her literary honors include fellowships from the Guggenheim Foundation, the Radcliffe Bunting Institute, the National Endowment for the Arts, and the Massachusetts Artists' Foundation. She lives in Cambridge, Massachusetts, with her husband and their son.

KAREN KARBO is the author of the novels *The Diamond Lane* and *Trespassers Welcome Here,* each of which was named a *New York Times* Notable Book of the Year. Her work has appeared in *Vogue, Esquire, Outside, Entertainment Weekly,* and the *New York Times.* She is a past winner of the General Electric Foundation Award for Younger Writers and a recipient of a fellowship from the National Endowment for the Arts. She grew up in Southern California and currently lives in Portland, Oregon.

ALEX KOTLOWITZ is the author of *There Are No Children Here: The Story of Two Boys Growing Up in the Other America*. The book was the recipient of numerous honors, including the Helen Bernstein Award for Excellence in Journalism, The Carl Sandburg Award, and the Christopher Award. It was also adapted for an ABC television movie of the week by Oprah Winfrey. A former staff writer at the *Wall Street Journal*, Kotlowitz has also received the Robert F. Kennedy Journalism Award, The George Polk Award, and the Catholic Interracial Council of New York's John LaFarge Memorial Award for Interracial Justice. Kotlowitz grew up in New York City and now lives in Oak Park, Illinois.

CLINT McCOWN is the author of the novel *The Member-Guest* and two volumes of poetry—*Sidetracks* and *Wind Over Water*. His stories have appeared in *Sewanee Review, Gettysburg Review, Denver Quarterly, Writers' Forum, Mid-American Review, Colorado Review, American Fiction, Northwest Review,* and elsewhere. He has twice won the *American Fiction* Prize, as well as an Academy of American Poets Prize, a Wisconsin New Work Award, an Associated Press Award for Documentary Excellence, and the Germaine Brée Book Award. He was born in Fayetteville, Tennessee, and lives in Beloit, Wisconsin.

SUSAN POWER is the author of the novel *The Grass Dancer,* winner of the PEN/Ernest Hemingway Foundation

Award for best first fiction of 1994. She is a graduate of Harvard/Radcliffe, Harvard Law School, and the Iowa Writers' Workshop, and the recipient of an Iowa Arts Fellowship, James Michener Fellowship and Bunting Institute Fellowship. Her short fiction has been published in *The Atlantic Monthly, The Paris Review, Ploughshares, Story,* and *The Best American Short Stories 1993.* Born and raised in Chicago, she currently lives in Cambridge, Massachusetts, where she is at work on her second novel, *War Bundles.*

ESMERALDA SANTIAGO is the author of *When I Was Puerto Rican,* a memoir. Her work has appeared in the *New York Times,* the *Boston Globe, The Christian Science Monitor,* and *Vista* magazine. She is a graduate of Manhattan's High School for the Performing Arts and Harvard University, where she was graduated with highest honors. She has an M.F.A. degree from Sarah Lawrence College. With her husband, director Frank Cantor, she owns CANTOMEDIA, a film production company. They have two children, Lucas and Ila, and live in Westchester County, New York.

MONA SIMPSON is the author of *Anywhere But Here* and *The Lost Father.* She is the recipient of the Guggenheim Foundation Grant, the Hodder Fellowship at Princeton, the Bard Center Fellowship at Bard College, and the Whiting Writers' Award. Her short stories have been selected for *Best American Short Stories* and the Pushcart Prize. Her new novel, *A Regular Guy,* will be published in 1996.

JANE SMILEY is the author of eight works of fiction, including *The Age of Grief* (which was nominated for a National Book Critics Circle Award), *The Greenlanders, Ordinary Love & Good Will, A Thousand Acres* (which won the Pulitzer Prize in 1992), and, most recently, *Moo.* She lives in Ames, Iowa, with her husband and their three children.

SALLIE TISDALE has written several books, including *Talk Dirty to Me, Stepping Westward,* and *Harvest Moon.* Her work appears in numerous magazines, including *Harper's,* where she is a contributing editor.

BAILEY WHITE teaches first grade in south Georgia and is a commentator for National Public Radio's evening news program "All Things Considered." She is the author of two books, *Mama Makes Up Her Mind* and *Sleeping at the Starlite Motel.* She is currently at work on a novel.

. . .

SHARON SLOAN FIFFER teaches English and writing at the University of Illinois, Chicago. She is the author of *Imagining America,* which was selected as one of the best one hundred books for young adults by the New York City Public Library in 1991. The former co-executive editor of the literary magazine *Other Voices,* she has received several honors for her short fiction, including the Illinois Arts Council Award.

STEVE FIFFER is the author of several nonfiction books, including two collaborations with Morris Dees, founder of the

Southern Poverty Law Center: *A Season for Justice,* which won the Christopher Award and the Gustavus Myers Award, and *Hate on Trial,* which was selected as a *New York Times* Most Notable Book of 1993.

The Fiffers recently coauthored the book *Fifty Ways to Help Your Community: A Handbook for Change.* They live in Evanston, Illinois, with their three children.

# ACKNOWLEDGMENTS

*Home* is a true collaboration. It could not have been built without the vision of Gordon Kato, the support of Sonny Mehta, the guidance of Sarah Burnes, the patience of our children—Kate, Nora, and Robert Fiffer—and the artistry of its eighteen remarkable contributors. We are grateful to all.